"U.S. LBM is leading the way, unleashing the wisdom, talents, and motivations of its team members to create a new type of company that is prepared to rethink everything. In this must read, L.T. shares this compelling story that you'll want to use to catalyze change, transformation, and innovation in your own business."

Dirk Beveridge

founder of UnleashWD and author of *INNOVATE! How Successful Distributors Lead Change in Disruptive Times*

"L.T. Gibson is the Happy Warrior of LBM. In my decade of reporting on construction supply, I'm hard-pressed to think of anyone else who's as infectiously upbeat, yet competitive. In just a few years, he has built and led a remarkable company that has become a prototype for our industry. In his book, Gibson delivers both an explanation of how U.S. LBM has come so far so fast and lots of good reasons why you're likely to continue to see this company continue to soar."

Craig Webb

editor-in-chief, *Remodeling* and *ProSales* at Hanley Wood

THE STORY OF US

THE STORY OF US

How the Culture at U.S. LBM
Is Changing the Distribution Industry

L . T . G I B S O N

Published by Advantage, Charleston, South Carolina.
Member of Advantage Media Group.

ADVANTAGE is a registered trademark and the Advantage colophon is a trademark of Advantage Media Group, Inc.

Printed in the United States of America.

ISBN: 978-1-59932-706-8
LCCN: 2015960636

Book design by Matthew Morse.

This publication is designed to provide accurate and authoritative information in regard to the subject matter covered. It is sold with the understanding that the publisher is not engaged in rendering legal, accounting, or other professional services. If legal advice or other expert assistance is required, the services of a competent professional person should be sought.

Advantage Media Group is proud to be a part of the Tree Neutral® program. Tree Neutral offsets the number of trees consumed in the production and printing of this book by taking proactive steps such as planting trees in direct proportion to the number of trees used to print books. To learn more about Tree Neutral, please visit www.treeneutral.com. To learn more about Advantage's commitment to being a responsible steward of the environment, please visit www.advantagefamily.com/green

Advantage Media Group is a publisher of business, self-improvement, and professional development books and online learning. We help entrepreneurs, business leaders, and professionals share their Stories, Passion, and Knowledge to help others Learn & Grow. Do you have a manuscript or book idea that you would like us to consider for publishing? Please visit advantagefamily.com or call 1.866.775.1696.

To Wyatt, Hayden, and Amelia,
for giving me the inspiration
to get better every day,
the courage to take chances,
and the ability to dream.

TABLE OF CONTENTS

ACKNOWLEDGEMENTS

The release of this book is met with mixed emotions. There is a part of me that fears readers may think I am arrogant and boastful. But, the truth is, this book isn't about me. It's the story of our amazing team— the story of US.

The stories and examples that make up the book come from the bold and courageous work of our people. I am so proud of our associates, many of whom are long-time industry veterans who have changed their mindset over the past few years and broken free of the paradigms and perceived barriers that no longer exist in our new business model. I am energized by the newcomers on our team who did not grow up in the lumber industry and who aren't afraid to bring their diverse perspectives and past experiences to our industry and our company. Lastly, I welcome the young generation of millennials who are looking for a great place to grow a career; we welcome their energy, initiative, and their will to make a difference.

Thank you to the corporate team who believes in the model. Although it is much easier to create SOPs, detailed policies and handbooks, and corporate mandates, it's not the way to unleash our collective productivity, innovation, and sustainable results. You breathe energy into the operating companies, which helps make the collective US so great.

Thank you to the division presidents, most of whom are previous Owner/Operators. I made a commitment to each and every one of you when you agreed to sell your business. I said we could work together to make your company stronger while providing a better future for your people. As long as I'm leading this company, I promise I won't let you down. In return, I depend on you to continue leading your division forward. Never settle. Push the limits. Embrace all the resources U.S. LBM has to offer, and I'm confident the performance will exceed your wildest imagination.

Thank you to each and every associate who dedicates their time and talents to U.S. LBM. We believe in you, and we appreciate all that you do to make US great! No matter if your job title is sales manager, truck driver, load builder, operations manager, HR, accounting, etc., you have the ability to continuously improve our business, our processes, and our service to customers. If you have an idea of how to make things better, speak up! We want to hear from you. You are empowered to make change!

I would be remiss if I didn't send a special thank you to Wendy Whiteash. This book simply would not exist without her. She epitomizes why the U.S. LBM model was created, and I am grateful everyday she is on our team.

I am proud to share the Story of US, and I hope all our associates take great pride in being a part of the story. Never lose sight of our vision of being the best! Take more risks; it's ok to fail, as long as we learn from the failure. Change is imminent. Be the disruptor, not the disrupted. We're just getting started!

ABOUT THE AUTHOR

L. T. Gibson has been president and CEO of U.S. LBM Holdings, LLC since founding the business in 2009. In that short time, U.S. LBM has grown to become one of the largest building-products distributors in the United States and the recipient of the 2015 ProSales Dealer of the Year award. U.S. LBM is an employee- and culture-driven company with over two hundred locations in twenty-four states. It is recognized as the fastest-growing company in its industry.

For over twenty-five years, L. T. Gibson has overseen multiple start-ups, integrations, and turnarounds for both small and large companies in the industry. He believes that a company should care for its employees first so they can better care for the customers. Creating the right culture, driven by trust and empowerment, enables employees to realize their full potential. The end result is a business hyperfocused and responsive to customer needs that ultimately improves faster than its competitors.

INTRODUCTION

One of my earliest jobs was mowing grass on a horse farm. I remember weed whacking along the farm's black board fences for miles a day. I was fourteen, so you can imagine how my mind wandered during such a mundane task. But rather than getting bored, I tried to set goals like finishing one-and-a-third miles by lunch or completing two-and-a-half miles for the day. When I achieved a goal, then I'd try to beat my record. That summer, I ended up making more money than the other three people that started the season with me. That's when I decided that, if you're the best or most productive at anything, you can be successful, feel good, and make more money.

That outlook has guided me my entire working career, and was the reason I left a multi-billion-dollar organization during the recent housing downturn to start a new company.

Today, I am president and CEO of U.S. LBM Holdings, LLC. Founded in 2009, U.S. LBM is a collection of leading building-material distributors across North America operating over two hundred locations in twenty-four states. The company's primary focus is on customers that require specialized services, such as custom homebuilders and professional remodelers as well as multifamily and commercial contractors. At the writing of this book, U.S. LBM is the third largest building-products distributor in the United States.

Our model is to serve as a platform for further investments and acquisitions in the pro-dealer market—preferably in partnership with current ownership/management. U.S. LBM encourages those individual businesses to operate as autonomous local divisions while enjoying the capital and other resources of a much larger national organization.

But what makes U.S. LBM different is our culture.

I've written this book to share our culture and our operating philosophy, because we truly believe this is the future of our industry.

If you're a U.S. LBM associate or partner, I'd like you to get an even deeper understanding of our culture; I want you to better understand why we are the way we are, and that we're going to constantly change and get better. I'd like for you to know that you make a difference, and that we appreciate everything you do. And if you keep challenging yourself and challenging us on how we do things, we're going to end up being what we want to be—the best company in our industry.

If you're a new graduate straight out of business school, I'd like for you to see exactly how much opportunity exists to change our industry. That's a pretty bold goal, but I believe that more opportunity may exist here than in any other industry—precisely because things have remained unchanged for so long.

If you're one of our competitors reading this book or if you're from another industry, I'd like you to see that there's a different way of doing things in the business world. If there was a standard that really worked, we'd all learn it in business school, and then we'd all operate the same way. In our industry, building and distribution, the perfect company doesn't exist yet. That means whoever achieves that is going to have to do things differently than we've done in the past. And that's what we're trying to do.

CHAPTER 1

THE BEGINNING OF U.S. LBM

People ask me all the time: What made me decide to leave an executive position with a multi-billion dollar organization during the worst housing downturn in our lifetime? The reason is that I had an epiphany in a hotel room in Indianapolis in early 2009. I had been given marching orders to shut down some of the historically most-profitable operating units in the company in order to free up capital to chase the trend of new housing permits south across the Sunbelt.

In the years leading up to 2009, I'd proudly led a vibrant region with hundreds of smart, talented, and loyal industry professionals in places like Wisconsin, Connecticut, New York, and New Jersey. Now they were being shut down or sold. We didn't have a significant presence in the Sunbelt, and I knew it would be an uphill battle. All our competitors had the same idea—to chase the housing permits—and competition became fierce, quickly eroding profits. In any case, the mandate to shut down profitable units didn't make sense to me.

My epiphany was this: success is about having great people with the right products and services in the right markets—that's where we should invest! That night, I had a phone call with my boss and I told him I was resigning.

After resigning, one of the first steps I took was to decide on a company name. While the name "U.S. LBM" may hold little significance for some, it really sets the stage for the rest of our story.

I found an article on the Internet that said a good name for a company tells "what the company is about" and "what the company does." So I drew a line down the middle of a notepad, and on the left side of the line, I listed all the things our new, fledging company would do. At the end of the day, I decided, we were lumber and building-material distributors. That's where the "LBM" came from.

Then, on the right side of the notepad, I listed ten or fifteen things to describe what the new company would be about. The first word I wrote on that side of the page was "us." I wanted this company to be about the people, and I defined those people as our employees, our vendors, our customers, and the residents of the communities where we help build homes. After originally incorporating the company as US LBM, it was later changed to U.S. LBM to signify that we are willing to go anywhere—not just the midwest—to partner with the right business. To me, the "U.S." still means "us," and signifies that we're in control of our own destiny—we control the pace of change and how we innovate our company to continue serving customer needs while creating value.

During the first few days after U.S. LBM was formed, I and other founders of the company sat down to lay out on paper our mission and vision and the basic tenets that would guide decision-making within the new company. We came up with five philosophies that we decided best represented what we wanted to build our company on. These philosophies remain deeply ingrained in our culture today:

People. We realize the value of our associates and partners and treat them with integrity, candor, and respect. We recognize that to be truly successful and provide our customers with world-class service, we must have satisfied associates. This, in turn, breeds customer loyalty.

Partnerships. We treat our vendors and customers with care and respect, because we understand the value of these relationships. What we do is a people-and-relationship business and our goal is to foster these partnerships and use them to enhance our successes.

Operational Excellence. This is at the core of our customer-value proposition. We maximize the value we give to our customers, vendors, and partners. By sharing best practices with all functional areas and across state boundaries, we expect to become the most profitable team in the industry.

Improvement. Our model is built on a foundation of efficiency and continuous improvement. By eliminating hierarchy within our organization, each of our companies operates in the manner that best services the local customer base. We will not allow "better" to get in the way of "best" as we continuously improve operations, setting the standard for which our competition is judged.

Empowerment. We empower our companies and associates to constantly improve. The foundation of this process is accountability and candor. Through commitment and determination, we will increase our value to our stakeholders and partners.

In October 2009, with our new name and philosophies in place, I and a handful of loyal friends who believed there was a better way than shutting down or being part of a one-size-fits-all company, formed U.S. LBM Holdings, LLC. We were fortunate to have the backing of Black-Eagle Partners, an operations-focused, middle-market private equity firm that seeks to acquire companies with sustainable business models that exhibit compelling future prospects.

We decided that the traditional company structure wasn't a good fit for our culture, so we set out to get the benefits of size while still maintaining a local and connected feel. Instead of a top-down business model, where everything looks, acts, and feels very similar, we went with a "decentralized corporate office," which supports the underlying businesses. (I'll talk about what I mean by "decentralized corporate office," or as I preferred to call it, our "entrepreneurial model," in the next chapter.) We do it this way because the companies we own all have long histories—they've been in business an average of eighty years—so they're good at certain things. They may not all be good at exactly the same things, but it's very easy to take best practices from one to the others.

In fact, we are inspired by the companies we acquire; we partner with them to make them better, but we also learn from them and share their best practices with other divisions—and everyone wins! We hold some of the best-known brands in the industry and see ourselves as stewards of those brands. So our efforts to help them become even better involves sharing metrics across the enterprise and giving them resources that maybe they haven't had in the past because they were small or independent.

We want to help our companies grow the business, but we don't believe they all have to be the same. Each company has its own culture, and we don't try to replace that. But while our companies retain their independent names, U.S. LBM doesn't feel like a lot of companies that are just banded together with common ownership. It looks, acts, feels, and moves like a single company with a single vision.

U.S. LBM's role, as we see it, is to try to enhance each company's culture with one that really lets people engage. That's our competitive advantage—to get everyone thinking about how we get better, how we do things differently across the company, what advantages we have over our competition, and how we turn our weaknesses into strengths in the years to come.

A lot of companies make the mistake of managing to the average. For instance, we have more than two hundred locations and it would be easy to say that, for X metric, the average in the company is X, and we want everybody to get there or better. But we don't do it that way. Instead, we try to rank our companies in order (from one to two hundred, or more, depending on the number of companies), and then we see what works with number one. But maybe what works with number one won't work in every market, so then we look at what works with the number-two company. Then we try to drive everybody toward number one, or number two, or whatever is the best fit. But more importantly, we try to challenge whoever is number one to get better! For example, if number one also did what number four does, number one might get even better. We try to get the people that are out in front to move forward even faster, thinking that the herd will keep up.

So we're not about trying to force some kind of a standard on any company when it's not going to fit. What we are about is finding great practices and applying them wherever we can to help move everybody move forward faster. We want to hear ideas and see who can get better the fastest.

All of the companies that we've acquired are outpacing growth in their markets. That's really the job of our "corporate office," such as it is. We partner with a company because it's great at, say, three out of eight things. As for the five things it's not as good at, we're going to help strengthen those things by bringing in ideas from the other companies. We don't make these people feel like we're micromanaging them or that we're top-down. We really are just going to help them get better and support them.

ACCELERATING OUR CULTURE

So the U.S. LBM culture is one of change and continuous improvement. From a planning perspective, we focus on culture and vision probably as much as we do anything else inside the company.

We really believe that culture matters! It dictates how decisions are made at a local level when we're not around. If you've got a culture of people who believe in what you're trying to do, it really makes the day-to-day management very simple. We all know what we want: we want to be the best company we can be, we want to get better faster, and we want to be innovative. All of those things speak for themselves. And to have the right mix of those things, you've got to have the right people.

Our culture really supports people who are entrepreneurial, competitive, and who have been successful in the past. It's pretty easy to take that subset of people and put them in our environment and watch them thrive. We take what they're really good at already and try to create an environment where that remains their strength rather than becoming a weakness or something they have to change. And then we really turn them loose with more resources, training, and capital than they had when they were a smaller company. If there's a secret sauce to what we do, that's it; we take what these companies are already really good at and let them grow and thrive, freeing them from whatever constraints they may have had in the past. We want our companies to retain their local flavor, in large part because of the local connections they've already established. Our customers range from national and regional builders to smaller builders that construct a couple of houses a year or even remodelers that have only one or two employees. Whatever their size, all of our companies and customers feel very connected to the local community, and they're constantly thinking about who the people in their marketplace are and how they live. Since everything happens in the local market and it's a very relationship-driven business, companies that have been successful in the past are the ones that really excel at continuing to build relationships with their local customers. And because they are entrepreneurs themselves, the leaders of these companies understand very well what it's like to own a business, to grow it, and to pass down to their associates that sense of pride in the company and those traits in how it acts and reacts.

So our role is just to enhance what is already taking place in the local markets. We want customers to continue to recognize those established brands, to keep the relationships they've had with local salespeople, and to know who to call when they've got a concern. I've been in this industry for twenty years, and I've seen what happens all too often when the acquired company has to implement all new procedures and rules—how it really causes employees and the former owner to disengage. And when a former owner leaves a company, you're left with managers running the business rather than people who feel a sense of ownership. That's not our culture; we want people to feel like owners of the business.

A PASSION FOR CHANGE

It's a different mindset when you create a company because you want to change the industry—because you want to change the dynamic of how you interact with vendors and with customers. It almost gives you a sense of freedom when you know that's what your company is about. And when it comes to the people who work for the company, that mindset really has nothing to do with age. Whether they're two years from retirement or twenty, everyone who works for U.S. LBM can buy into what we're doing and how we're trying to change things.

I used to believe you only change things that you felt could truly make you better. Now, even if we get the same or better results, I think we're willing to change because we enjoy the journey. Every time we change something, we learn so much more. We try to create a culture where it's okay to fail, because even when we fail, we've learned so much. It helps us the next time that we try to adjust to fix that same problem. We know so much more than we did before. People putting themselves into a business and putting themselves out there is the most important part of creating a vision and creating a culture.

Our company's culture is one that doesn't fear failure, even though the fear of failure and of change is huge in today's society. Still, I think most people are more comfortable if they understand why they're changing and what the end game is in those changes. Once they realize that the change isn't designed to do something negative, then they don't feel so much like they're going down a road that's unknown to them. So we create ways for people to see where they're going so they feel much safer as they make those decisions and go through those changes.

CHAPTER 2

A CORPORATE CAMPUS WITHOUT WALLS

U.S. LBM has no physical corporate office. We're a group of thirty people, but there is no building labeled with a "U.S. LBM" sign where all thirty of those people show up every day. Instead, corporate employees work in remote offices but spend most of their time working with leaders of divisions around the country.

So, of course, we're continually asked how we operate without a bricks-and-mortar corporate headquarters.

For the purposes of explanation, I'll use the word "decentralized" to describe our "corporate office" structure. But I prefer the word "entrepreneurial."

It's easier to go out and raise capital to start a new business than it is to actually create a strong culture and compelling vision for a business. Under a command-and-control structure, it's generally a very small group of people, or maybe even one person, at the top of the organization who comes up with the strategy, policies, and standard operating procedures. Those are typically driven down through layers of regional, district, and market managers with little concern for the impact on front-line process workers or on customers and vendors. That is the opposite of what U.S. LBM is all about.

We have turned that whole hierarchical structure upside down. We, the corporate staff, work for the divisions. Individuals on the executive team aren't tied down by boardroom meetings, random office drop-ins, or watercooler chitchat because we are working in operations spread out across the country in New York, New Jersey, Chicago, Philadelphia, Detroit, and Atlanta. We regularly cross paths in the operating units and meet formally every thirty days or so in hotel boardrooms or restaurant meeting rooms, which symbolically transform into the U.S. LBM corporate office for that day.

Dale Carlson, president of Lyman Companies, a U.S. LBM operating company, describes how the model works from his point of view:

> The presidents and senior leadership team communicate via a biweekly conference call and generally get together quarterly. With no central office, meetings are moved around the country to the different operating companies. When in town, you are encouraged to tour the local operating company to gain and share best practices. Members of the U.S. LBM corporate team live in three different time zones, so e-mail is probably the easiest and best way to communicate with them.

Instead of having one person on top of the hierarchy with a team of six to fifteen senior executives responsible for "managing" all the assets of the company and setting strategy in isolation, we have five-hundred-plus associates helping run our business. They are continually improving processes at every level of the organization, and always striving to find the next big idea to change our industry; we believe that every one of our associates is just as capable of coming up with the next big thing as anyone at the corporate level.

This decentralized, or entrepreneurial, business model was not put in place by accident. It was designed to support the core values of the organization without being overbearing. As I touched briefly upon in the previous chapter, the role of corporate is not to "micromanage" the day-to-day operations of the local operators. Rather, the role of each corporate staff member is to bring best-in-class resources to those operational groups so that they win in their respective market. And by "win," we mean "be the best."

Our corporate office staff is constantly out visiting our locations, which is another part of the reason we don't have a physical corporate office. We want them out there visiting operations so that they can see and gather great ideas that are then shared across the enterprise. They can also visit with the groups and subgroups that exist in our organization as well as help challenge ideas and promote conversation throughout our organization.

Obviously, this is a different model from our competitors. But we just believe that command-and-control no longer works. Antonio Rossano, president of East Haven Builders Supply, a U.S. LBM operating company, explains some of the benefits of this corporate structure:

> The fact that there is no overarching physical corporate presence, in my opinion, makes the operating company intrinsically more independent and in tune with the markets. We know that there is help up above, but only if needed. Unlike most corporations, U.S. LBM's corporate structure is more a

collaborative effort than the kind of corporate dictate that is often viewed with skepticism and suspicion by the associates. The U.S. LBM structure instills a sense of belonging, which is not common in companies of this size.

Again, we want our companies to continue to feel unbelievably close to the customer, and to be thinking about and acting on ways to improve the customer's world, instead of focusing on the demands of a corporate office or a corporate entity. So you're not going to see a lot of egos at the corporate-office level. If we stand up in front of the group and we talk about a good idea, the people in that group are going to act on it because it's good for the business and it helps make a better company. Honestly, I can't recall an opportunity where everybody hasn't really jumped in to make corporate strategies work in their local markets—because they all feel like they have a voice in the decision. That's really powerful, especially for somebody who's owned a business for a long time. If other presidents can see the benefits of a particular decision or strategic direction, they'll be knocking down the doors to get onboard.

We call this "sell don't tell." Outsiders often overuse the adjective "autonomous" to describe the relationship between our divisions. We act like a single company where it makes sense—in purchasing, for example. Or in specialty product lines. That's why we really don't have difficulty gaining buy-in and alignment to leveraging our collective size because joining forces on "back offices" processes just makes good business sense in many cases.

With no formal corporate office, we work on the basis of essentially just knowing where we are and whom we're dealing with each day. For some people, I think it's a little unnatural at first to work in this kind of environment. But once they understand how it works, it's really empowering—it's fast-paced and exciting.

Scott Converse, director of process-improvement programs for the University of Wisconsin-Madison School of Business, has been our lead instructor and project mentor since the start of our partnership with the University. Here Scott comments on our quick and agile decision making, including what it was like getting started with us on a professional-development program:

> In every continuous-improvement or general-management course, you hear phrases thrown around like "actionable decision making" or "data-driven decision making." You hear statements like "Develop a culture that supports your customers and your employees," or "A failed initiative is not failure if you learn and adapt." But unfortunately, many organizations are unable to apply these common-sense thoughts in a positive way. I've seen U.S. LBM apply actionable decision making from the highest leadership level all the way down to newest front-line worker. I've seen how they have continued to foster a culture that embraces positive change while still supporting their workers at all levels, and I've seen them grow and thrive. And the whole time having fun along the way—incredible!
>
> I knew U.S. LBM was different the first time I met with the leadership team. For many organizations, making decisions on the role of professional development is a long process. The meetings are preceded by a series of emails with long waits, followed by multiple con-

ference calls, and more waiting. Then others within the organization are inserted in the loop and we go through the activity again. This vetting can take over six months.

Not with U.S. LBM. After an initial ten-minute call with very directed questions, the leadership team said, "We'll fly there and have you show us examples." We met later that week and after the walking tour and meeting, they asked for some privacy. After five minutes, the decision was made, and we then quickly began design work to help them with professional development. What a refreshing change!

Operating like this can be a little difficult on people working at the corporate-office level, particularly if they have a controlling personality. In traditional corporations, it's easier on the people operating in the corporate-office bubble if everyone out in the field operates in the same way. It's much more difficult to manage multiple locations if the people in the field all do things differently. In fact, if you have a controlling personality, it'll drive you crazy to work in the office and not know what's going on all the time. We're the opposite. When we hire people, we sometimes need to spend a little time working with them trying to drive that controlling mentality out of their personality.

We don't put much stock in job titles or job descriptions at the corporate level because we have a flat hierarchy and no silos. I won't say we're quite to the point where we can eliminate titles altogether, but everyone on the team knows they are empowered to make decisions in the best interest of the operating units and our customers. We want every one of our associates to freely interact across divisions, product lines, and functional areas. I want every customer to feel like anytime he or she is talking to someone in our organization, he or she is talking to an owner who can make decisions. Nothing makes me crazier than to have an environment where employees have to tell customers, "I've got to check with corporate" or "Corporate policy says I can't do that for you." The only way to ensure none of that happens is to do away with unnecessary policies and empower people to make decisions locally.

We spend a lot of effort indoctrinating new hires into the U.S. LBM culture very quickly. Obviously, we need the right fit—people who can work autonomously and be comfortable with communicating via technology instead of in person. We make major business deals every day using technology, including email, cellphones, and even texting. But I think we probably communicate better than most people in a corporate office because we don't have to stand in doorways waiting our turn or waste time hunting someone down for an answer.

Too often, people spend time in their daily lives on things that don't necessarily add value. In the U.S. LBM environment—a company so large with so few people at the corporate level—everyone has so much to deal with that they learn to prioritize very quickly. Decisions have to be made every day, usually at a pretty rapid pace, and priorities become apparent very quickly. Things you thought were important last year you're probably not even doing this year, because in that short amount of time you've come to realize that you only have time to focus on the most important thing. I think that is a hard concept for a lot of people to grasp, especially people who feel like they have to check every box, every day.

So we want our corporate people to focus on the big picture and let the people at the local level execute. Which is the opposite of what most business books teach—to make a plan and assign strategies. But once you prioritize and make decisions based on what's going to make the biggest impact, it's actually kind of liberating. You don't feel guilty that you haven't gotten to everything, because you're taking care of the most important things first.

The point is, while we operate on a nontraditional model, we look act and feel more like one company than any other I have seen. How? Because we are aligned in where we are going and the tools we want to use get there. We are aligned in vision, culture, and values. The rest is just employing consistent actions to back up everything else.

ELIMINATING SILOS

The U.S. LBM culture eliminates the silos of the past, where people worked in small, independent groups focused on a specific processes embedded within such areas as order taking, purchasing, or delivery without understanding how their work impacted upstream or down-stream stakeholders. In today's competitive environment, where everyone must understand how we're all connected, we must eliminate those silos.

We do this by taking every opportunity to communicate the U.S. LBM vision to all associates. A vision that is known by few is not very valuable to an organization. If you've got a powerful vision that you truly want to implement, everybody in the organization has to under-stand that vision and buy into it. They need to clearly see how their personal role in the organization fits into the overall vision. They must be able to understand how to define success and failure in what they do.

The most important job of any leader of any business, at any level, is really to communicate the vision to their people. Vision creates a safety net that allows change to occur. Without change, obviously, there's no innovation. The two are connected. You have to communicate a vision to your people so they know what they're changing, and why they're changing. Clear, concise, and frequent communication of the road forward enables change to happen at a faster rate. It also helps all the managers throughout an organization. If they can see exactly what the vision of a company is, the day-to-day decisions become very easy. Is the decision consistent or inconsistent with where we're going?

When you think about it, our industry hasn't changed that much since the beginning of the 1900s; other than replacing the word "horse" with "truck," not much is really all that different. But change is coming—fast—because we have the technology and the same ability to change as other industries out there that have already done so. It's an exciting time to be in our space and doing what we do, and I'm excited to see what we do tomorrow.

I love our slogan, "Accelerating at the Speed of US," because when you really think about it, it comes down to the people. We can either use the past to limit what we think and how fast we move forward, or we can open our minds and go forward at a speed that we never dreamed possible. If you put the right people in the right culture, it can be an amazing thing to watch.

CHAPTER 3

TRUST AND EMPOWERMENT

In order to successfully implement game-changing technology, create new and innovative processes, and develop complex systems to track data, a strong culture of trust and empowerment is absolutely required. That's why people are the key to the success or demise of our organizations. Our secret to success is creating the right culture and having the right people in that culture. When you have those two things, it's pretty amazing what a business can do. Really, the sky is the limit. The old-fashioned command-and-control, ego-driven model in today's environment just moves too slowly to stay competitive.

So, what does the "people-first" mantra mean at U.S. LBM? Many companies, large and small, contend to put people first; but putting people first is about more than just words on a poster or a website. At U.S. LBM, it's how we treat the people who work throughout the organization. We want to be very progressive, and move fast, but we know to do that we have to have the right people inside our culture. We must have people who are prepared and want to make decisions—sometimes very tough decisions—each and every day. And we arm them with tools and resources to be successful. In addition, we treat people with courtesy and respect, and we strive to make associates feel good about what we're doing as an organization. We need them to trust the direction and trust the U.S. LBM vision so they can buy into the entire process.

Caring about people was one of the key tenants I and the other founders wrote down the day we created the company. In order to treat our customers better, and truly understand their unique business needs and challenges, we must have associates who are engaged and who feel we have their backs as a company. We want associates across the country to feel we are very connected and responsive. To do that, we must be a people-first company. We have to take care of our associates and look out for them so that there's no doubt we're there to support them as they face the challenges that occur naturally with change.

Antonio Rossano, the East Haven Builders Supply president, explains it this way:

> The corporate culture at U.S. LBM is based on values of service and accountability. From my experience as a founding member, these concepts are enhanced by empowering a local feel. The end result makes the whole effort unique in its capacity of being nimble and responsive to local needs."

Empowerment breeds confidence and conviction. It lets people know they make a difference and that you are looking out for their future. When the pressure heats up, we simply stay focused on what's important. We focus on the customers to make sure we understand their needs and deliver with reliability. When all those things are done right, the morale is higher, and people can do a better job because they are confident and happy. Empowering our employees makes us feel closer to the customer. It makes all the difference in the world to have people who are fully engaged in the company and who want the company to do well. I'll put a company with engaged employees who feel like they make a difference up against a company that doesn't empower its employees any day of the week! And that first company will win.

Speed is another advantage. By trusting and empowering our people, we can make decisions quickly. Our people aren't afraid to make decisions and do the right thing for customers. We really view our vendors and customers, and this is because we honestly view our vendors and customers as our partners. Our job is to help make their businesses better, and to do that, we've got to have employees who really think about their value to the customer. Each one must think: "How do I make my customers' jobs easier, help them build faster, and help them create more value for their customer?" There's a tremendous amount of loyalty to our company from the people that operate in it because they love how we function, and they like the feeling that they matter.

Trust and empowerment are also essential when building a company willing to take risks and try new things. When people say they love the company they work for, what they're really talking about is the culture. So we try to make sure that we have an environment that people embrace. That way, we achieve associate buy-in around change. This then inspires associates to get involved and help to drive the change, rather than be naysayers—or worse, try to sabotage change. When our associates understand that the company is built on the premise of "us," then it's easy to grasp that we can move forward at "the Speed of US." It's a strong metaphor we use to reinforce the ideal that anyone, any individual in our company, can drive change and drive us forward. We strive for every associate in our group to feel like he or she owns the improvement of this business.

I often let people know that they got this job because of their attitude, knowledge, and experience. And then I let them know that, now that they are an U.S. LBM team member, they can begin thinking differently. I want them to know that they no longer have to worry about managing up, down, or sideways. There is no box for them to worry about getting out of. And there are no boundaries on what they can get involved with. I tell them they not only have the *ability* to make a real difference, but that is exactly what is *expected* of them.

We want people in the company who have a "spark," something different that makes them want to be the best and get better. Then we find programs, training, mentors, discussions, support, tools, walks on the beach—whatever it takes to help those people feel confident, safe, and free enough to let all that spark out to where it impacts their job.

This also drives innovation. Innovative thinking occurs when people feel like they're in a safe environment, where they're equipped with the tools and knowledge to think creatively, and empowered to share those ideas upward. If you have 4,500-plus people who are invested in fostering an innovation mindset, you don't really have to put many resources behind it. You don't need a dedicated team to innovate. When your whole company is innovating, it's much more powerful and valuable.

It's amazing where ideas can come from—and that's why we try to give everybody the tools to innovate and change. The bright ideas can come from any part of the organization. It's truly rewarding as a leader of business—or as a partner to these people—to see what we can accomplish together. And we need *all* of the superstars this industry has to offer: the people who are great managers, forklift drivers, truck drivers, purchasers, estimators, and everyone else. We need all of them. Sometimes, if we're lucky, we find industry people who are experts in their field and also have a real passion for constantly making things better. When we join forces with that type of person, watch out for the fireworks!

LETTING GO AS LEADERS

When it comes to empowering people, I think it's hard for leaders to let go and trust that others will make better decisions than they might. This can be especially true with leaders who maybe have more experience or a different mindset than the people they are leading. But I believe the more you can let go, the more you see that the company is better off because of it.

I tend to find myself leading more like a coach than a decision-maker. In group situations, I don't see myself as necessarily always having the best ideas. My job, I believe, is to challenge the ideas that are brought up and to help people really use their own experiences to find a better answer. They know their jobs better than I know their jobs. So whatever the idea might be, I'll often try to take the opposite stance just to make that person think about why their idea is great. His or her idea may actually be the best one in the room, but I'll try to poke holes in it just so we can flesh it out and make it even better—because we don't want just a broad idea, we want the best idea. And the best way to get that is to challenge it. Maybe we can come up with an even more outrageous solution than anybody's ever thought of before.

If you think small, you end up with small, incremental improvements. Sometimes to challenge us to think bigger, we'll throw out an absolute and work backwards. For example, to get a team brainstorming about improving inventory turns, I asked them to picture a lumberyard without any inventory. Just-in-time inventory would be achieved when all of the product we receive in a day is turned around and shipped back out to the customer in the same day. To up that thinking, I asked if we could think of a way where we're so good at logistics that we don't need trucks at all? Could we schedule things to go through some other mechanism?

In our business, of course, we can't do either one of those things. But after I let the group squirm a little with that unrealistic challenge, I got them to realize that although the absolute may not be possible, there are certainly valid ideas to get us closer to that utopia. Could we achieve zero days sales outstanding (DSO), pulling inventory for shipment as soon as it is received into our system, and then shipping it and billing the customer in the same day it was received? Or if zero DSO is impossible—essentially showing no inventory on our books—could we achieve DSO of one day, two days, or three days? I don't know the answer. But, by encouraging people to start digging into the idea, I could take them all the way to one extreme and then let them work back to where the realm of possibility may be.

So again, I think the job of a leader is to help people think bigger than they typically would. It pushes people out of their comfort zone and helps get the creative juices flowing to think to the extreme. When their minds are free to think bigger, then what was impossible yesterday might be possible tomorrow. You get more robust answers, and instead of making incremental movements, you move in leaps and bounds.

Often, people in an organization think they are restricted by the resources that they have or by the idea itself. But what really restricts businesses are the people at the top. Too often the people at the top focus on one or two ideas at a time, and they send that focus down throughout the ranks. They watch how those one or two ideas evolve and then move on to the next idea.

There is a time to focus on efficiency and a time to focus on the big steps forward. We have the ability to take two-hundred-plus "rifle shots" at a time and pick the most effective to roll out to the broader group where they would be most effective. So we don't want to be good at creating rules, but we want to be great at getting better and focusing on the big moves and leaps forward. By nature, people fill in the procedures and rules on their own. If you focus instead on the rare qualities of risk-taking, disruption, and rapid changes from new ideas and opportunities in your culture, you will truly differentiate yourself from others. At the same time, you create an environment where people are excited to be involved.

So what's amazing with our model is that, instead of focusing on those one or two ideas formulated at the top, we can focus on ten or twenty ideas because we've got so many people who feel like they have a say in the company. Those of us in the "corporate office" are not the gatekeepers, but rather we are the facilitators. We add value by letting people do more, which allows us to try different strategies and improve multiple things at once. If we had the traditional structure of top-down management, I don't think we would be able to keep up with that pace of change. Instead, we've seen every metric in the company go forward and be positive. There is still plenty of room for improvement, but if you benchmark U.S. LBM today against major competitors in sales growth, earnings margin, and net profit margin, all of those trends are positive in comparison. That's a testament to the culture and to the model—but more importantly, to the fact that we engage and that the people in our company want to get better.

It also helps that we are not just a five-year-old company. We're really an eighty-year-old company when you consider all of the companies that make up U.S. LBM. Everything we do ends up with a better answer than we started with because of the people we have onboard and the focus that we have on really improving and finding new and better ways.

Outsiders are usually surprised to hear my perspective that getting people to embrace change has not been as challenging as they might assume. It seems to be a general assumption by leaders that most employees are resistant to change. Our experience has been quite the opposite. Since we have provided people with the tools and a work environment built on trust and encouragement, it has been amazing how many people have bought into change. Then, as we celebrate the small and big wins along the way, it inspires them to be more proactive about driving change in their location or department. I've seen associates advocating for change who I would have never dreamed could break out of their traditional perspectives. I've known some fifteen- or twenty-year industry veterans in our company who I now see acting totally different than they did in the past.

It's really because the culture is different than anything they've experienced before. They feel safe. They feel they can make changes, and really do some exciting things. Regardless of age, gender, or anything else, we've got all kinds of people driving new initiatives in the business. It's so refreshing for me to see.

I think you do yourself a great disservice when you set a goal that is an industry standard and then just make little tweaks that work toward that number. Maybe you actually achieve that goal, but then guess what? It's not over, there's still tomorrow. Just because the industry says X is success, doesn't mean, in our book, that it's the best that *can* be.

We've got examples in our company of many off-the-chart metrics—and those come from exceptional people trying things. We believe if you can constantly challenge yourself and make those big leaps forward, then you can end up in places that you never believed you could get to. And that happens when you empower people to make change.

Bill Imig, president of Wisconsin Building Supply, a division of U.S. LBM, says the company's culture is similar to a small, close-knit family business with a primary goal of providing outstanding customer service and a focus on building relationships, working on continuous improvement, and being a leader in the industry. Imig has been in this industry thirty-five-plus years, but he doesn't allow the past to limit what's possible in the future.

"Our U.S. LBM structure has allowed me to focus on the issues that impact Wisconsin Building Supply without getting bogged down by the corporate bureaucracy that many large companies experience. Although we operate somewhat autonomously, like a small business, the resources in the technology area that are available to us due to the size of U.S. LBM have allowed us to provide outstanding services to our customers and excel in many areas. Our state-of-the-art systems in logistics, purchasing, customer-relationship management, design, and estimating software, along with our customer app, have helped make us a leader in our industry."

CHAPTER 4

ALL HANDS ON DECK

Our goal at U.S. LBM is to be a very collaborative team. It really is an "all-hands-on-deck" approach.

We don't mind people having pride in what they do, but big egos don't work in this environment. When we see maybe too much ego showing, whether it's in a person or in a meeting, collectively we challenge that way of thinking. Over time, people with too much ego get left behind in our company because they get stuck in the old ways and/or have too much pride in what they *used* to do. People who are willing to accept new ways of doing things get better faster, and when their numbers outshine the others who are stuck in the old way of doing things, then those people who are stuck in a rut really feel the pain of watching everyone else move ahead.

It starts pretty much as soon as someone is onboard. When people first join the team and they begin to understand the model, they sometimes test the system in small increments. Once they figure out they can trust the system, that they can try new things and fail, then some of them keep going. And again, to be able to operate the way we do, they've got to embrace that other people have ideas that are better than theirs. You can't be a controlling person and still also get everything moving forward. You've got to involve others or you'll never be able to do all the things you need to do to get better at the same rate as everyone else in the organization.

CONSISTENCY IS KEY

Here are five points I impress on leaders in our company. This is a message I have been consistent about since we incorporated in 2009. At the time, we were a $200 million-dollar company in three markets. Today, we're a $2 billion-dollar-plus company in twenty-four markets across the country.

1. **Our associates come first.** I know this may seem odd with every business saying the *customer* is job number one and that the *customer* comes first. But I truly believe that our *associates* should come first in *all* of our decisions. They are the most important part of our teams, and we serve them. This doesn't mean they should be overpaid or given too much leniency. It simply means that we recognize that to truly be successful and treat our customers the way we want them to be treated, we must first treat our associates in a way that lets them know how highly we value and appreciate them. The most powerful emotions in our business are pride and happiness. I want our people to be proud of what we do and how we do it and happy that they are part of our team. I want them to truly enjoy what we do. This concept needs to permeate everything this company is about—from safety to every procedure and every policy. So again, while our ultimate goal is customer loyalty, that begins with associate satisfaction and caring.

2. **Operational excellence.** Simply said, we will get better every day. We will share ideas across locations and markets and strive to run the most efficient, highest-performing teams in our industry. Period.

3. **Partnerships.** Much like our associates, our vendors and customers will be treated with care and respect. We understand the value of these relationships and will treat them accordingly. This is still very much a people and relationship business. It is our desire to foster these partnerships and use them to enhance our success as well as the success of those we partner with.

4. **Speed.** Our entire model is being built for speed in the marketplace. No political hierarchy, no lengthy chain of command. See opportunity, evaluate actions, act—it's that simple! Picture a group of frogs sitting in a meeting talking about how to find some food, then picture one frog that snaps up everything flying by almost without thinking—got the picture? We say this a lot, but we will prove how true it is: "It's not the big that eat the small, it's the fast that eat the slow."

5. **Accountability and candor.** This will reinforce many of the first four points, but we must be very specific about defining success and discussing issues and problems with candor and, in turn, holding all of us accountable. In his book *How to Think Like a CEO and Act Like a Leader*, Michael F. Andrew says, "it's best to treat issues coldly and people warmly." That's really it. If you see a problem, don't beat around the bush—address it. Feedback is the most important tool in learning. Picture a coach in any sport at practice ... constant feedback all geared at improvement. It's never mean or personal, it's

about getting better. It's the opposite of being disappointed in someone—it's actually a demonstration that you care about that player and his or her success. We simply are going to be the best. And to do that, we must define what that looks like and hold each other accountable for doing our part.

THE IMPACT OF COLLABORATION

To move really fast, you have to be able to consider how your decisions impact others. For example, when I talk to the executive team at U.S. LBM, I'm not worried about them managing the day-to-day functions of what they're in charge of. Whether it's human resources or finance, operations or sales, or whatever the function might be, my question to them is: "What have you done this year, this month, this week, to make the two-hundred-plus locations better?" What are we doing in each market to make them better? That's what I care about.

Setting that tone for the team results in a collaborative discussion. Nobody gets caught up in his or her own silo because everyone realizes they need cooperation from different areas of the business to really make a difference. Our leaders are out in the field every week visiting associates and sitting in on sales and operational meetings to better understand the opportunities for growth. Because they're all very in tune with the local businesses, I'm just as likely to ask the chief financial officer or the directors of learning and development or information technology to get involved in an operational issue. I don't "manage" the executive team based on decisions that they make or how they managed a particular situation or a function. I manage them based on how much they are improving the business, how much they are helping to share best practices from one group to the other, and how much progress has been made on driving agreed-upon priorities.

To promote collaboration, incentives and compensation across the corporate staff and division operations are based on overall performance, not on specific markets. Since we all share in the company getting better, our incentives are very much aligned with the way we talk, look, and act. When one person/division gets better, it helps us all get better. I believe this compensation philosophy helps drive the team to be open-minded and supportive of one another.

While looking for areas to improve the business, we don't let "better" get in the way of "best." We think of "average" and "status quo" as very bad words in our culture. When we benchmark, we benchmark across the group. I mentioned before how it's easy to manage to the average and say, "Wow, everybody is below average, but if this one division were just average, we'd be great, so let's raise that one division up." But, as I said, we don't do that at all; we benchmark everybody and we focus everybody on number one. We closely examine what number one is doing differently. Then, we ask ourselves, "How can number one be even better?" We spend a tremendous amount of time with number one to see how much further we can push that division. We spread that message of how they do it and help everyone understand that there are different ways—better ways.

SPREADING THE MESSAGE

True collaboration takes a tremendous amount of communication. We promote discussion in several ways. One is through affinity groups, in which we bring together various roles in a division to share best practices, current challenges and opportunities, subject matter expertise, and so on. Affinity groups are more than just department meetings—they are opportunities for peers to interact across geographies and business units. They include, for example, monthly sales-manager calls, quarterly president meetings, monthly human-resource-manager calls, product-line-manager quarterly meetings, manufacturing/plant-manager meetings, and so on.

We also have an annual meeting where we communicate specific priorities and initiatives for the next year and where we remind everybody of our overall vision. In this meeting, we intentionally put groups of people together to facilitate communication. We have Green Belt presentations that put project leaders "on stage" so other operating company presidents and peers can hear about projects, what was learned, how to leverage the idea across locations, and so on. And through our new U-Connect social learning network, we're able to connect people through online technologies.

When we get a group together for a meeting or other function, the first thing we do is make sure we take a little time to reinforce the culture and the vision.

Granted, outside of our gatherings, it isn't always easy to communicate a vision—due to how spread out we are and the fact that many associates are on the road or in the field. So sometimes we need to get creative to get our point across. For example, in the quarterly U.S. LBM newsletter, *Building Connections*, we have a section called "Ask L.T.," which addresses questions submitted by associates. We get lots of questions about business- and non-business-related topics. There are enough questions that I can't address them all in the newsletter, but I really enjoy hitting on the points concerning our vision, and why we're different, and how this model works. Since our model is harder to execute, sometimes people question if it can be scaled as we grow. Or sometimes they argue that it would be easier to just tell the divisions what we need them to do. And they're right. It *would* be easier for the corporate staff to hand out mandates and dictate processes and policies. To be honest, when we created the model, we weren't really sure how it would work. But now we're believers that the easy way isn't the best way. And, we want to be the best.

We also conduct focus groups with customers in the local market. And in each market, we hold strategy sessions to share our progress and provide transparency throughout our operations. In these strategy sessions, we focus on things like where we are today, the things we're the best at, the things we're not the best at, the things we need to develop strategies around so that we become the best, and opportunities that we see in the future because of the way the industry is evolving. We really tailor these to each market because our reach is vast enough that there are differences. Typically, we'll also address some overriding opportunities that we have to capitalize on.

But these strategy sessions aren't once-a-year gatherings where corporate swoops in and starts dictating what the local operating company should do. We're there to uncover innovative ideas that create value—game changers that we can expand across the group. We can take these strategies to the next quarterly meeting and say, "This is a real difference-maker. This is that operation's before and after, this is what they did, and this is how they did it."

HEALTHY CONFLICT

Early on, the small group of "us" agreed that it was important we all hold each other very accountable for what we do. It's a built-in mechanism to remind ourselves to stop and assess. It's never personal, but rather a way to remind each other of our key tenants.

While I expect everyone on the team to curb their egos and to communicate in an open, honest, and respectful manner with each other, I don't want a bunch of "yes" people surrounding me. Healthy conflict with a strong sense of ownership and accountability makes companies thrive. We lay all the ideas out on the table and help each other to make the right choices and move us forward. And we're okay with ideas being challenged. But we don't want to just challenge what people say; we want to challenge what we've done historically and what our industry or other industries have done.

It goes back to communication: we have to be able to communicate what we want, why we want to do it, and how it's going to make things better. Ensuring thorough communication on the front end has helped us facilitate positive change.

CHAPTER 5

OPERATIONAL EXCELLENCE

Second to being a company about people, we are a continuous-improvement company. The more successful we can make our customers and our vendors, the more successful we become. That's U.S. LBM's role—to make the entire supply chain better!

Innovation is what we've found drives all things forward. It's about how we embrace technology, how we bring other industry best practices into ours, and how we're constantly trying to find a new secret sauce to make something that we're doing better. If we can get out in front of our competition and continually make ourselves better, then eventually we'll end up with very little competition.

In our entrepreneurial model, there is a really wide swath on how exactly to take the road forward. The key is that we're all on the same road, and we're all moving forward. Our methods of inspiring others to embrace change are also a significant part of our overall culture. Since we are determined to change at a rapid pace, we must be capable of doing so. Therefore, not only do we want to change as quickly as our competitors, but we want to go as fast as technology and the innovations of today will allow us to go.

So we go out and look for new innovations and technology. That includes looking at other industries because we find there is much to be learned even outside our own marketplace. We're constantly evaluating best practices in other industries to examine how we can apply those ideas in our own business as a way of helping us continue to generate value for our customers, our vendor partners, and our associates.

Randy Aardema, U.S. LBM executive vice president of supply chain, explains how we've implemented processes from two other industries:

> L.T. encourages us to use improvement techniques from other industries and apply them to ours. For example, we use a NASCAR pit-stop process to enhance our truck-turnaround process. And we combine this with "changeover-reduction" techniques developed in the manufacturing industry to help define the turnaround-improvement process. Then, of course, we provide performance measures to let everyone in the company know who is best and where to go to get best practice ideas.

So, when we look at other industries and apply their best practices to our own industry, we ask questions like: How do we simplify a complex process or relationship? How can we make a current process or service work, look, feel, and act better? A lot of times, the answers are simply to innovate, change, do things differently, get better. Our customers' businesses are changing—just like ours. So how do we help them meet the changing needs of today and tomorrow?

MAKING LEAPS WITH TECHNOLOGY

In a commodity business like lumber and building materials, data rules. Some of the highly guarded data in our business includes cost, sell price, rebate dollars, margin percentages, and so on. We've gotten so protective of those critical pieces of information that in many cases we've "hidden" information that really doesn't need to be protected.

When we started the company, we partnered with the right enterprise resource planning (ERP) systems. But in order to gain significant advantage in the industry, we felt we needed to implement more than just a new ERP system. Through the process of constantly challenging ourselves, we decided, "Why not just give customers everything we can see?" Rather than us keeping all the information to manage our business to ourselves and our customers having to call to obtain answers to questions, why couldn't we give customers a conduit to see all of their information themselves—just like we do— so they don't have to call in all the time? So that's what we set out to do. We didn't know if we'd succeed, but we knew we had to try. Ultimately, we connected our ERP system and our distribution software, and then linked it real-time to customers so they can see exactly what we see every minute of the day.

In our effort to make our customers' lives easier by being more transparent, we took a great leap of faith and created our own mobile application. We get inspiration from the things we love in our daily life—the tools we use and depend on. I travel every week, so I fell in love with the Delta Airlines app because of its simplicity; it let me do everything I needed to do. I didn't need to call other people, and I could rely on myself to make the change. So we modeled a lot of the functionality of our mobile app after the Delta app. It's simple and clean.

With our app, we put in the hands of every customer everything we know about the supply chain. We provide real-time access to product receiving and delivery times, along with photos of the product as soon as it hits the jobsite.

> *Our mobile app project captures the soul of our culture. The vision for the app and many other key initiatives were developed mostly through midnight email exchanges with L.T. He felt it was the right thing to do for our company and customers, and the biggest investment in 2014 was approved in no time by Rick. Just like that! We do what's right, and we do it fast. That's why we are special. We truly accelerate at the speed of US.*
>
> *— Senthil Arumugam*
> *vice president of distribution, U.S. LBM*

We take all the information that we have, which most people probably view as sacred data for managing their business, and we give it all directly to our customers to help them do their jobs more efficiently. We've giving them the tools that normally only our inside sales reps and dispatchers have.

What we saw in the application was the ability for everyone, us and our customers, to have information at their fingertips. It allows users to feel more connected to the company they're dealing with, and for customers, it feels like the service the company is providing is much better. Even though they're not actually talking to a person at the company, they're able to retrieve information themselves in real time.

In the distribution business, customers are constantly calling to see where things are and what time their deliveries will arrive so they can schedule their subcontractors. The app gives people information about where trucks are, what's on them, how the routes are being run, whether they are ahead of schedule or behind schedule, what's in each shipment, and so on. It has far exceeded our expectations in not only how clean and easy it is to use but also in how customers have embraced it. Many of the users are people who might not normally use much technology to run their businesses, but because it's so easy to use, it has really become a game changer for our customers.

I mean, it's just unbelievable how receptive customers have been, and it's growing exponentially. Currently we have more than one thousand regular mobile-app users, and each user interacts with the app on average about five times a day. That means they're not just logging on to see what's happening in the morning, but they're using it throughout the day to see what's going on, what's where, and to schedule things with their subcontractors. So they're actually using the information from the app to manage their jobs, and that's exactly what it was created for. It's a great tool that is creating more efficiency in the channel and in the industry. By helping people to schedule things tighter, there's much less wasted time.

But we didn't stop at just offering a real-time look at our supply chain. In one of our focus groups, a customer said, "You know, when I have that information, it's great. The first thing I do is open up messaging and I send a text to my subcontractors to tell them the products are on-site." To which our vice president overseeing the mobile app project quickly replied, "I think we can do that *for* you."

So we created a message button on the app. As soon as the product is offloaded at jobsites, the customer is notified by text. He can simply select the message button, and a text is automatically written, for example: "Last two windows were delivered at 10:17 a.m., pictures are attached." He just selects the button, his contacts pop up, he chooses who he wants to send the text to, and he presses "send." With essentially three clicks, he sends the text to all of the people that need to know the product is on-site.

Think about how much wasted time and how many wasted resources have been eliminated by the mobile app. Without the app, a customer would call a salesperson for basic questions like, "What time is a shipment being delivered?" The salesperson would then call dispatch or an inside salesperson. So, a couple of phone calls for every one of those instances is being eliminated. Given that we have over one thousand users accessing the app each day on average five times, then that's five thousand calls per day that are eliminated for non-value-add questions. Not only are those calls eliminated, but customers feel better about the experience.

I know that when I go in and change my seat on the Delta Air Lines app, not only do I save a phone call or a trip to the kiosk that I had to make in the past, but it's so much faster that I feel better about Delta because they let me do that myself, very quickly. It creates loyalty, and it creates a competitive advantage. A customer of ours using our app can manage three or four jobs at once; without the app, they were only able to accomplish half that much.

I think our app also creates a sticky relationship and loyalty; imagine how frustrating it would be to become accustomed to having the app and then having it taken away from you because somebody decided to switch suppliers. And that's exactly the intent, to find ways to create value in the channel.

As a relatively new company, the real advantage of our technology platform is that it is fairly new, up-to-date, and very accurate. So the technology has been a real game changer for us as well. But even though we feel like we've got a competitive advantage with the app, we don't want to stop there. We want to know how customers are going to want to function and connect with somebody tomorrow.

The app has been an eye-opener for us. It's been enlightening. We want to do more of that. We want to be more of an open book in both directions to help both of those groups—customers and vendors—become more efficient. We've learned that providing transparency doesn't diminish our role as a valued partner, but it actually enhances it.

In addition to the app, there have been other key decision points thus far that, quite honestly, were a big leap of faith given the capital investment required. Considering our meager beginnings, we could have gone cheap with our ERP system. But instead, we went out and got what we thought was the best ERP system at that time. Its functionality is robust, yet its interface is clean and it's simple to use. On top of that, we put in place a best-in-class logistics platform. Then, we made it even better by creating automation to make sure that our mobile app would work the way we wanted it to.

Of course, the cherry on top was our investment in creating our own mobile app. Beyond the impact it's had on our own business, I think it's a game changer in our industry because of the amount of information we're putting in the hands of customers. I think those decisions—to keep things clean and simple and yet be innovative, and to put the newest-possible technologies out there—are things that are going to probably reap the biggest benefit for us.

IMPLEMENTING TECHNOLOGY

Technology by itself is not very compelling. If you take the technology and create a more seamless way to manage a business and share it with customers, that's when it can be exciting.

For instance, the mobile app is just one example of how we've focused on making sure our customers can do their jobs in a simpler, more efficient fashion. As innovative thinkers, we're constantly thinking of new ways to do things, and when we brainstorm and experiment, we do it in a very focused way—the mobile app was born out of that spirit of innovation.

So having access to technology is only part of the equation. I think we have to stay true to ourselves, and whenever technology lets us get better, then we'll implement it.

Looking forward, we will all have access to constantly improving technology. The ability to take some of that technology and weave it into your business where it makes sense and creates value to your customers will be the real challenge. A lot of people who spend a lot of money on technology don't do a great job of implementing it with their team in order to ensure that it works as intended. Consequently, they miss an opportunity to get the real value out of that technology. With so many choices in technology solutions today, it's a challenge for every company and every leader to decide exactly where to invest time and dollars.

You never know what's next, but whatever the new technology, I believe that how you integrate it will be the key to success. Those who implement best will win. If you find technology that enhances how you operate, or propels your brand image, figure out how that technology integrates with your other business processes. Otherwise, the new technology won't be accepted or sustainable.

We have a lot of confidence that whatever the next big market disrupter is, we're prepared to act quickly and embrace whatever change is needed to thrive. We're going to be as good, or better, at the next big change than anybody else in our space. We are preparing every day by constantly changing and improving what we already have control over. When the next big disrupter arrives, we'll know how to handle it. I can already envision the management meeting in my head. We'll be saying something like: "Wow, here it is. We knew something like this was coming. Now, let's put a team together. Let's go out and make sure that we do it better than anybody else."

One way we prepare is through Lean Six Sigma and Kaizen events. I'll discuss these in greater detail later in the book, but these are activities that have helped us look at our processes and do things to turn around or reorganize to make our operations more efficient. To be clear, U.S. LBM doesn't have a corporate "Lean Team." Rather, we teach and empower associates on the front lines—the local markets—to continually make improvements in their areas. There is a great sense of pride and accomplishment when associates personally identify and then work through projects on their own. The return on investment is immeasurable when you consider the three-hundred-plus associates working on local improvement projects at any given time across the enterprise.

There is no beginning or end to our continuous-improvement drive. It's constant. By the time we get an improvement plan implemented in one place, hopefully somebody else will have raised the bar even higher. It's a continuous focus on making processes and services better for us and all our stakeholders.

CHAPTER 6

CREATING VALUE FOR EVERYONE IN THE CHANNEL

Everything we do is based on our value proposition and how we approach our customers, vendors, and associates. Every decision takes those groups into consideration. But what I've found in defining a value proposition is that it's not massive moves to the left or right that differentiate one company from another. Rather, it's just little things you can do to make someone's life better—whether that's trying to make a customer's job easier or trying to make life better for someone in need in the community.

At the end of the day, what U.S. LBM is all about is creating value for everyone in our channel. Again, when we define the construct of our channel, we're talking about the vendors we buy products from—the makers and distributors who supply our companies. We're talking about our companies—the businesses that we have acquired; these are typically wholesale companies that sell primarily to the building professional, although some of our organizations are retail operations. And we're also talking about the customers that we (our companies) sell products to. These are typically professional builders—national, regional, and custom builders; remodelers; and even some do-it-yourselfers.

Our value proposition is something we focus on more than most, I think. And we do it in a unique way: we look at the value we can create for our customers and our vendors in the supply chain. We think about who we buy from, who we sell to, and how we create more value for both of those partners. Plus we try to consider how we can help vendors become more efficient and profitable, while at the same time helping our customers be more efficient and profitable. That's how we improve upon our service levels. It's how we fill the channel.

We always start with listening to the voice of the customer. Then, as we strategize on how we can make our vendors more profitable, we do so with the expectation that they will be able to provide better service to our account in return. Perhaps they can even offer better pricing to take to market, because their cost to serve is lower with U.S. LBM. Sometimes the answers mutually benefit each other in surprising ways, creating a win-win across the board.

If we can create value in both directions, we'll be very successful at what we do. It will make us not only the preferred path to the market for the vendors, but also the preferred place to buy products for our customers. That's really what we strive to do—to create more value for everybody in the channel, which ultimately includes ourselves.

R. Hunter Morin explains what makes U.S. LBM different when it comes to relationships. Morin is president and founder of The GeMROI Company, a national marketing agency in the building-materials industry, and co-founder of The Jian Group, an investment-banking organization that has become one of the most active mergers-and-acquisitions firms in the building-materials industry. As he puts it:

What makes U.S. LBM different is the same thing that makes the company successful—the strongest possible leadership, with a caring attitude about associates and customers. It's unusual for a company like U.S. LBM to have the same caring attitude toward suppliers. U.S. LBM does that better than anybody in the industry. The company values relationships, understands the value of relationships at all levels, and builds on these relationships.

Many companies pay lip service. The leadership of U.S. LBM and all of the acquired companies, at least those with which we are familiar, understand the code of success, the value of independence, and the strength of association. It has been fun to watch.

THE SCORECARD WITH VENDORS

For a lot of companies, dealing with a vendor is strictly about negotiating price. But one of the unique and collaborative things we do with vendors is to create sales plans. As the customer, we try to push the price down while the vendor/manufacturer tries to push prices up. So we try to create a more equitable sales plan that looks at what we sold this year through a location and what level we want to take those sales to next year, along with how we specifically intend to make that happen. We'll designate who owns each of the projects, what kind of support the vendor will get from us, and how we'll *all* share in any gains.

As we grow bigger and we gain more leverage on pricing, we don't take advantage of that by creating an adversarial relationship. Rather, we create true joint strategies for growing our vendors' product in our markets. Participants walk away from those meetings with key assignments or an understanding of what their role is. The vendor-strategy meetings are critical because we identify, together, where we need local-market product development or some help coming up with a new product, especially if it's a competitive situation.

When we name a vendor of the year, we talk about the sales plan we've created and look at how the vendor executes its half of the plan. For example, maybe the vendor has committed to sales associate training or taking new products into new markets. We look at how we execute on the growth strategy together and how they measure up "on-time" and "in-full" to our locations. That means getting the material there on the exact day and time that we expect—not a day early, not a day late—and also completely shipped, so that we can meet our commitments to our customers.

We also look at the representation the vendor has in the field. How responsive is the company to issues? How does it handle joint sales calls with our people?

With our key vendors, we talk about our growth plan together: how we're going to grow sales for their specific product in our locations, how we can expand into other markets, how they can execute on the plan, and so on.

Most of our key vendors really like this support because it's unique. We all want to grow. And together, we can usually come up with some interesting plans. Every year, the plans get better and better as we learn more about each other.

Again, price is obviously important, but it's not the only criteria to consider when choosing a vendor partner. Since the real game changer in our business is figuring out how to make our customers more profitable, we look for vendors who can help our customer go fast, build better, or create a competitive advantage with their product. Then together, we will sell more.

We don't always partner with the biggest manufacturers. We like companies that are more progressive and more innovative. We try to partner with those companies because they give us the impetus to continue on our path. It allows for a great opportunity to share ideas and discover how we can work together to create a more efficient channel.

Quality is another big part of our vendor scorecard; it's the way our customers judge us, so obviously it's a top priority. The reason we deal with our specific vendor manufacturers is because of the quality and the perceived quality of their products. We would never compromise. If we thought anything was substandard or if they had a lower ability to produce the kind of quality that our customers expect, we just wouldn't deal with that vendor.

Key elements of our vendor scorecard are year-over-year sales growth and market-share growth. These are important because if both we and our vendor consistently outperform the market, everybody is happy. But it is an interesting irony that we don't mandate the operating companies buy or specify products from preferred vendors. Our philosophy is that we provide the products and services our customers want to buy. So we put together a joint business plan for how to best promote, sell, and earn the customer's business through marketing, merchandising, and service support. The plan also benchmarks important elements such as timely delivery, excellent quality, and a superior value proposition. The results of our vendor partnership approach have been very successful and a marvelous departure from the old, adversarial gamesmanship techniques.

— Randy Aardema
executive vice president, supply chain, U.S. LBM

When we're vetting vendors, our decisions are heavily weighted on past experiences through our companies. We use internal data that our companies have gathered to review each vendor's reputation and how well known its brand is. We look at the efficiency—how quickly and regularly vendors can get us the product: Do they ship on time and in full to us so that we can fulfill our commitments to our customers? Do they have any advantages on frequency of delivery? Do they support our sales structure? Do they have support in the field? Do they have product knowledge in the field? Can they do training for our salespeople? We look at quite a checklist of things they do for us that add value, much of which is beyond price.

CREATING VALUE WITH CUSTOMERS

What we do upstream with our vendors also works downstream with our customers—just as we spend time improving our value to our vendor partners, we also do the same exercises with our customers.

Our customers want us to understand how they create value for their customers or their shareholders. They create value by the services they provide to customers (i.e., the homeowner or property owner). So we spend a lot of time figuring out how we can be a better partner with them to help them do their jobs better. We see our job as helping our customers communicate better with their customers, and helping them be more efficient in answering questions or solving problems for their customers. And, that's how we define being a good partner in today's changing market: helping our customers create value for their customers.

We try to add value at every step of the chain for our customers through things like product demonstrations, lunch and learns, and breakfast meetings where we go over new products or industry topics. If they need certain products in the showroom, we try to be very responsive every step of the way. Every year, we also spend a lot of time at each one of our units, talking to our customers about our value proposition and how we enhance that for each different customer type—whether that's a roofer, a builder, or a remodeler. How do we become more valuable to them in the future than we are right now? That typically means enhanced service, more back-office assistance, manufacturing components, and so on. We try to make sure we are everything they need from us and more.

But first and foremost, it's all about our shipments to them being on time and in full when they expect them so they know they can schedule things around us. Our reliability is what helps them be the most efficient builders or remodelers that they can be. That's really what our brand means to our customers. But now, it's not enough just to say, "Your product will arrive at seven o'clock Tuesday morning." It's also about saying, "Not only will the product be delivered at the time promised, but I will notify you when it has arrived, and I'll make it easy to notify your subcontractor or homeowner that it's there." People in the channel also want easy access to warranty information and specifications to show how one brand compares to another. Providing this information at our customers' fingertips makes them appear more professional, reliable, and valuable in the eyes of their customers.

Customers like the fact that we are innovative and progressive, because it signifies that no matter what challenges they face, we're giving them best-in-class resources to manage their business. We're actually making their businesses better along the way.

At the risk of sounding arrogant, we want U.S. LBM to be the best. We want to be the best across every customer type and every product category in every market we serve. It's not arrogance, but rather, it's a personal drive—a fire in the belly to go beyond what we previously thought was possible.

Since we're constantly focused on being the best and adding value in each of those customer and product segments, we've become really good at measuring and benchmarking data around all the critical-to-quality factors important to customers. So, we don't have that "we're really good at service" answer. Instead, we can say, "We were on time, in full, 99.92 percent of the time for you over the last quarter."

At the end of the day, that's what our brands stand for. To be number one, customers need to rely on us and trust that we understand whatever they need us to do. Next, they need to see us as problem-solvers for their business. They need to know that we're good partners for them.

VALUE IN THE COMMUNITY

Just as we create value for vendors and customers, we also create value for associates and the communities in which they live.

Creating value for our own associates means the opportunity for them to have ownership in U.S. LBM. We feel it's very important that every associate feel connected to the company by more than just a paycheck, so we're creating a mechanism in which they can all buy shares and participate in the upside of the company.

Since our companies have been around a long time, we also feel like we are stewards in their communities. We feel like we've got a large associate, vendor, and customer population. And the stronger our company is, the more people we hire, the more people we promote, the better citizens they become, and the better they are in their local communities as well. So it kind of falls on us to make sure we do everything we can to help out the local charities—those that help people who are less fortunate or who are going through hard times.

One of the ways we create value is by giving back through the U.S. LBM Foundation. We created the foundation to ensure we're supporting charities and causes that make a difference—and that are important to us and to our associates. For instance, the foundation partners with the Wounded Warrior Project, the National Multiple Sclerosis Society, Habitat for Humanity, the Make a Wish Foundation, and Team Joseph to improve life for people in need.

WE'RE IN THIS TOGETHER

In this ever-changing business environment, we focus on the things that we know are constant. For instance, we invest time and energy with our customers to understand their priorities and their needs. And we get to know our vendor partners closely, engaging them by explaining our core values and strategic priorities. We want vendors to see us as the right vehicle to market for their products. And we genuinely see customers and vendors as our partners in growing the business.

We all need each other (suppliers, distributors, customers, customer's customers). I've considered the possibility of the disintermediation in the supply chain, and I can't imagine where that can occur anytime in the near future. Most of the manufacturers probably view us as an essential part of the supply chain. I know our builders certainly do.

When you're confident in the role you play in the supply chain, and you're certain you provide value, then you become more integral to the whole. For us, it also means becoming more open to the idea of sharing information that can make us all better partners. And that goes for our companies, vendors, manufacturers, customers, and communities.

CHAPTER 7

CATCHING LIGHTNING IN A BOTTLE

Hiring is another area where being intentional about "culture" makes a difference. In every hiring decision, we consider whether or not the candidate is able to operate within our decentralized culture with few silos and lots of dotted-line reporting. Is the candidate able to move our culture forward by taking risks and challenging the status quo? Can he or she achieve goals with no direct authority over operations? Is this person humble enough to book his or her own travel and complete his or her own expense reports—because we don't have a big administrative staff to do those tasks?

It's always a challenge to make sure we have the right people on the team, both at the corporate level and also with our company partners out in the field. Some people need daily directions or have trouble prioritizing on their own, and if so, our corporate structure really isn't the model for them.

But we think many people really *would* prefer a model like ours. People naturally want to be successful at their work; they want to go home feeling good about themselves. And the only way that happens is if they have some accountability and responsibility for their company.

Today, we read and hear a lot about *associate engagement*. There's no better way to get people engaged in a company than to make them feel like their decisions matter. If they want to wake up tomorrow and change the world with a great idea, we have a company that will embrace them. We're willing to try just about anything to get better. It's empowering for people to know that every day they can really make a difference.

We obviously want people who are open-minded and who are willing and open to change. And we don't necessarily just hire people from inside the industry. We're okay looking outside the industry for talent, because we always embrace new and better ways to do things. More than anything, we want people who want to get better, who are willing to take some chances, try new things, and who want to be part of a progressive company both in the use of technology and in our systems and processes. In short, we want people who are willing to think differently.

We definitely try to locate folks who desire to make a difference, who are not accepting of status quo. We want people who continuously look to push for excellence, who are willing to take risks, and who want to grow.

We want people who are willing to get involved and actually work with our teams and understand the business really well; we want the people who are willing to learn it from the ground up. We don't have too many people that aren't willing to pull up their boots and get to work. And we don't have people who can't put their ego in their back pocket—which keeps the politics out of the business as well.

GRANDPA WOULD BE AMAZED

To new hires, I have one message: This is not your grandfather's lumberyard. The industry has changed. Not only do we see ourselves as progressive, but we will become even more progressive in the future.

Again, I may sound arrogant when I say that joining U.S. LBM is an opportunity to change the world, but it's not a complete exaggeration. We operate in a great industry that helps families build the American dream. We're motivated by the challenges and disruptions in our industry because we're not just a group of people waiting around for the economic recovery. We're a group that's seeing a new day and a new industry. We're not only considering business solutions for today, but at the same time we're trying to create future disruptions in the supply chain that will result in our competitive advantage.

What we offer is the opportunity for people to be themselves, to go as far as they're comfortable going, and to be as progressive as they're comfortable being. If you want to be in an industry where you can have an impact and feel good about your contribution, feel connected to the company, and feel ownership in the company, then this is the place to be.

We can give people resources that other companies don't offer, from support to technology to industry knowledge. We've got a nice mix of talent in the company, and there are a lot of resources for people to use to do whatever they can dream up.

We find that it's something of a self-fulfilling truism that some leaders in our industry continue to say we're not an attractive industry. We're not going to be able to recruit young talent because this is not a sexy or attractive business. But we're doing our best to change that image. We're trying to encourage younger generations to explore our industry as a challenging and rewarding career opportunity.

At the end of the day, we're not just building homes and commercial structures, we're helping people live better lives. I've never seen an industry with so much opportunity for change and excitement, for changing things with new technology and outside ideas. It's actually a very fulfilling industry to be part of.

ENCOURAGING EXCELLENCE

Sometimes, as company leaders, we underestimate the skills and loyalty of our current workforce. We go out to the market to look for that perfect person or perfect leader to come in and save the day and take us to a new level. But I've found that if you put the right person in the right culture, that's really where you catch lightning in a bottle.

For instance, we did a Kaizen event as part of our Lean program where we started out just planning to reorganize one yard at one of the New York locations—nothing too sexy on the surface.

Little had changed with regard to layout in the yard for twenty or thirty years, even though equipment, products, technology, and product usage had all changed in that span of time. And the same was true for most yards in our organization and really across the industry.

In this particular yard, we engaged drivers, order pickers, and operational leads to take a fresh look at moving high-turning SKUs closer to a loading area and to stack things a different way to make room for new equipment, and as a result, we came away with more than the small, incremental gains in efficiency that we were expecting. We ended up making some monumental shifts in efficiency just by taking a fresh look. For example, we reduced forklift travel time by over 30 percent. The results of the event reinvigorated us and made us realize that we should look again at everything we do, including areas we don't believe need improvement. Since we've taken that new outlook, it's amazing what we've found in areas that we never dreamed held opportunity.

These kinds of advances really work if you just hire the right people, put them in the right culture, and then let them go out and change the business.

So again, we want our people to challenge the business. We're focused on having not only a great set of metrics for our business but also on constantly driving everybody toward best-in-class or even best-across-any-industry ideas. Our focus on constantly trying to find ways to make ourselves better and on helping our companies get better starts with having the right people.

If you find the right people and keep adding the right people to the model and then continue finding ways to share the vision, the culture just continues to get embedded deeper and deeper. Really, it can just mushroom because your people will drive the thing so far, so fast. It really at some point becomes amazing. It becomes easier and easier to go out and find the right partners to bring into the group to make sure that they make you better as you make them better.

A problem for our business, and across the construction industry, is America's current talent shortage. I attend many different industry conferences and roundtable discussions and one topic always comes up—how do we attract and retain talent? How do we attract millennials to our aging workforce, and how do we retain CDL drivers? Attracting talent to our industry comes down to one thing—culture! Do you have the type of culture that the most skilled people would want to work for?

I truly believe if I can convince any candidate to at least talk with us, he or she will see an opportunity to work in an exciting industry with promotion potential, tools for learning and improving the business, and a caring and supportive team of coworkers. I think if you give anyone on my team ten minutes with a prospect, he or she will convince him or her that U.S. LBM is the place to achieve anything that's possible—as well as be a part of something pretty special. That's the way we view it. That's the way we sell it. Because of our confidence in the culture, we've been able to attract talented people who may never have otherwise considered a career in building materials.

Again, people want to be a part of something bigger than themselves. They want to know their contribution makes a difference.

Sounds great—maybe too good to be true, right? We've invested millions of dollars in technology to make U.S. LBM different than our competitors. We've spent another million dollars in leadership and Lean Six Sigma training. Our company has doubled in top-line revenue in less than two years, providing nearly unlimited promotional opportunities for associates. When current and prospective employees see that we put our investment behind our story, they realize we're the real deal and different than what they may have experienced in the past.

And yet again, ours is not a work environment for everyone; it's not for people accustomed to working strictly eight to five or needing direction all the time. As I've said, it's constant, and it's fast-paced. Most of our people have a real passion for this business. And for them, it's not a burden to be at work.

Most of the time, I don't really view myself as being at work or not at work. But while we're "clocked in" more than most companies, there is a bit of freedom in our model, too. For instance, if someone needs to pick up his or her kids from school at three o'clock today, nobody in the organization would have a problem with that. Likewise, if someone needed you on a call at six o'clock, you would adjust and make time for that as well. It really is a model for people who know how to manage their time, to exercise self-control, to buckle down when they need to, and to take time off when it's needed.

As we consider the future workforce of millennials, it's clear they are a generation with many different career options. They want to invest their future in a company with a bold vision. They want to be a part of something bigger than themselves, and they want to know their contribution makes a difference.

When you absolutely love what you do, you don't feel like you're going to "work." When people ask me what I do in my spare time, I tell them that—if I have a choice—I do more of this, because it's what I enjoy the most.

CHAPTER 8

LEARNING AND DEVELOPMENT

U.S. LBM is a company that believes in continuous improvement, but we also know that we must give people the tools to execute those improvements.

When we created the company, we decided continuous improvement would be at our core. It's one thing to say that you stand for continuous improvement; however, it's quite another to really put something around it.

To support our model, we have made a significant investment in learning and development for all associates. Specifically, we have prioritized resources to be spent on Lean Six Sigma training, leadership development, and coaching and mentoring across all areas of the business.

We started this investment about two-and-a-half years after we founded U.S. LBM, when we created the US1 program, which is a road map for how we can get better in every area of the company. To date, US1 projects across U.S. LBM are expected to have a positive earnings impact of millions of dollars. And we're just getting started!

CASE STUDY:
DAYS IN WAREHOUSE

Led by Dave Pluth, information technology manager,

Lyman Companies

When it was discovered that cross-dock items were sitting in the warehouse at one U.S. LBM company for an average of 10.43 business days before being delivered to the customer, a Kaizen event was undertaken to resolve the issue.

There were a number of downsides to having items sit for that length of time including a negative impact on cash flow, overutilization of limited warehouse space, higher numbers of lost and damaged product that then had to be replaced, and problems with customer-fabricated required dates.

Procedures implemented as a result of the Kaizen event included employment of standard operating procedures for ordering of cabinets based on a required date; the installation of an automated mail notification system for past-due ship dates; proactive communication with customers to secure firm ship dates; and the addition of a monitoring system that displays historical and current days in the warehouse to sales, account coordinators, and management.

The results of implementation for a single customer included an account for one thousand cabinets per month and a drop in average days in warehouse from 19.67 at the start of the project in March 2014 to 6.31 in April 2015. Special orders now consume half the warehouse space, with an estimated annual savings of $40,500 in warehouse, labor, and finance charges.

CASE STUDY:
RECRUITING FOR RETAINMENT
Led by Scott Gertjejansen, Carpentry Contractors Co. (CCC)

While some continuous improvement projects may entail cost-cutting strategies, not all are undertaken with this objective in mind. In some cases, US1 projects may even incur costs at the onset.

Carpentry Contractors Co. (CCC) provides pro builders in the Twin Cities area with framing and trim carpentry labor, window installation, wall panels, prebuilt components, and more. At any given time, an average of 325 employed team members make up CCC crews. By its nature, this trade experiences a high turnover rate. To put this challenge into perspective, CCC hired 277 new employees in 2013; by 2014, only 146 remained. The cost of this turnover rate is significant in time and cost to find, hire, and train new employees.

After examining the situation, CCC implemented a more disciplined recruiting/hiring process that included a qualifying scorecard in an effort to consistently deliver a quality applicant and make CCC a magnet company. Although there would ultimately be additional costs incurred for training, the changes significantly reduced CCC's overall recruiting costs.

The changes implemented resulted in an increased retention rate of 23 percent. By developing a more stable, trained, and tenured workforce, CCC was also able to take on additional business and enhance existing relationships, resulting in increased sales revenue and earnings.

CASE STUDY:
SUDDEN INFLUX OF BUSINESS
Led by Dan DiGerolamo, IT operations manager and
Green Belt graduate, Universal Supply Company

As a result of Hurricane Sandy in October 2013, Universal Supply, located on Long Beach Island in Manahawkin, New Jersey, experienced an influx of contractor walk-ins. The increase in yard traffic created logistical issues and resulted in the delay of delivery trucks being unloaded, loads being built, and customers being able to pick up their products. Since the yard is gridlocked by marshes, expansion of the facility was not an option.

The solutions the team implemented included:

- installing racking to spread product vertically versus throughout on the ground;
- installing a warehouse-management system to shorten load times and eliminate the amount of time delivery trucks were in the warehouse area;
- instituting a designated customer pick-up area, as well as a separate vendor area, to better control and manage traffic, allowing incoming and outbound trucks to easily maneuver through the yard;
- creating a new yard layout by organizing like products in similar areas, eliminating the need for the warehouse team, customers, and vendors to navigate throughout the entire yard to build, pick up, or drop off orders;
- moving winter-buy products to another location.

CASE STUDY (CONT.)

As a result of the changes, the yard doubled its sales from October 2012 to 2014 with no facility expansion.

"Although Universal Supply has been using process-improvement strategies, we've never used the analytic precision that we learned through US1 training," said Dan DiGerolamo, Universal Supply's IT operations manager and a Green Belt graduate. "I understand now just how powerful putting scientific knowledge behind process improvement can be and what a significant impact it can have. I have a newfound respect for Lean Six Sigma."

The backbone of our continuous-improvement roadmap is the Lean Six Sigma training that we do in partnership with the University of Wisconsin. Through the multi-day training at the Fluno Center for Continued Professional Education and Development, participants learn a framework and the tools needed to analyze and implement sustainable changes that eliminate waste and add value. This program engrains in our culture the call to action to constantly challenge everything, to look at every process, to ask why, and to consider if there is a better, more efficient way. It also teaches us to evaluate data rather than make assumptions when we do a project. Also, it creates a discipline about measuring progress after an improvement has been implemented so as to make sure we continue to improve and sustain the gains we realized during the project.

The program is one of the ways we invest in people that empowers them to act. We didn't hire a corporate Lean team to go in and implement these initiatives. Rather, we teach our people how to use the tools, and we give them the resources and support to encourage them to make the change. It goes against our culture to bring in a corporate team to teach people how to run their businesses better. We even want our people to *identify* the projects. We believe the best ideas and practices are already out there, we just need to document them and share them across the U.S. LBM divisions.

For some companies, Lean Six Sigma carries many negative connotations. In many companies, "streamlining" results in loss of personnel and other ruthless cost-cutting. For us, it's the opposite. We're not taking people out of the system, but rather, we're growing so fast we need more people. And Lean Six Sigma really is about helping us get more efficient so we have more time to do the things that provide value for our customers.

Dale Carlson, president of the Lyman Lumber Companies, recalled some of the ways Lean Six Sigma has helped his operating company:

> The implementation of a Lean Six Sigma culture has been the most positive and significant improvement we have made at the Lyman Companies in the past decade. A couple of examples:
>
> Lean principles have been the foundation of the productivity gains at Carpentry Contractors Co. (CCC) in that there is a best way to frame a house. The CCC team continues to use Lean tools to analyze every framing process to drive out waste and improve cycle time. These improvements have allowed CCC to raise its productivity and at the same time offer customers a higher-quality product and a consistent customer experience.
>
> Our productivity gains have been significant in our paper processes as well. Using DMAIC (Define,

Measure, Analyze, Improve and Control) tools, we have defined and improved our accounts payable processes at our locations and general office. The improvements allowed us to move part of the accounts-payable process from the locations to our general office without adding any additional general-accounting staff.

From day one, it's been determined that it's not necessarily top-down who goes into training. Anybody who has the aspiration and the interest and the commitment to working on projects can go, from administration to salespeople to drivers to forklift operators. We send people at all levels and across all functions to the training because we feel like we can improve every part of the company. We want everybody in the company to have access to the tools. We want every part of the organization to focus on getting better and refining how we do things.

True, it's a sizable investment, but it's one that we're fully behind and willing to make because we see the impact it can have.

Lean Six Sigma helps the associates in our organization understand the impact they have on others. For instance, we address skepticism in the organization by putting a process or a function through the lens of a Six Sigma or Kaizen project. We do this in an effort to make it more efficient—to try to find a way of doing it better. By involving skeptics (who need a little more prodding to embrace change), along with their teams, the skeptics are not only going to hear from the people above, below, and beside them, but they're also going to see the actions of everything that they do. They're also going to hear ideas from the people all around them on how they can improve. I think that is probably the best way to open peoples' eyes to the negative impact that skepticism can have.

The Lean Six Sigma program is also a great way to celebrate successes and to recognize someone who is trying something different that's really working, someone who is making a positive impact. Since we document Lean Six Sigma projects, we can share successes we're seeing with everyone else across the organization. This gives us great visibility into what everyone is trying across the enterprise.

Personally, I always enjoy stopping in to visit with the Six Sigma Yellow Belt classes over dinner or cocktails in the Fluno Center Study Pub, because I enjoy the diversity and rich discussions that come from the participants. You may have a vice president of sales in the same class as truck drivers, loaders, salespeople, human-resources professionals, truss designers, estimators, purchasers, and so on. Quite frankly, we get a tremendous amount of feedback from participants that the experience not only changes the way they do their job, but it also changes the way they view their life. There is a sense of empowerment when someone who has felt stuck in a rut doing the same thing for five years discovers how to change and be in control of his or her situation.

For example, we have a CDL truck driver who recently attended a Yellow Belt course. He returned to his job fired up with what he had learned. He thought he could make an impact on truck-turnaround time in his yard. A team was gathered, and a Kaizen event ensued, which resulted in a 30 percent reduction of the yard footprint and a 30 percent reduction in forklift driving distance on typical loads. Now other locations are conducting the same Kaizen-style projects in their yards, and some have reduced truck turnaround times by more than 50 percent.

Other people see what a major impact one Kaizen event can make to a location, and they start to ask if they can go to class, too. All of a sudden, we have teams looking at all sorts of things, for example, the way we do collections and accounts receivable, or the paper flow through the accounts payable process, or how we can eliminate non-value-added steps in estimating, or reducing missed time-clock punches needed to process payroll. From there, the real magic happens when we find a really successful change, and we take that best practice and blow it out across the entire organization. We celebrate the team that has raised the bar for us all, regardless of their job titles. They get recognized, and it's very powerful.

U.S. LBM UNIVERSITY

U.S. LBM University is another level of training for associates in key positions or those who have shown the ability to differentiate themselves in our company. U.S. LBM University is a class on taking risk; it's a class on why we believe the things we do, how we're different, and what we're willing to do to really push forward the idea of being innovative and progressive.

Through the university, we take people who have shown a little spark and we fan the flame a bit and see if we can get them to turn into future superstars by taking chances, leading change, and showing a deep understanding of what makes U.S. LBM special.

What makes this class particularly special is that it's completely taught by our executive team. The commitment shown by the six or seven leaders who come together to teach it is really impressive. They see professional development as such an important aspect of our business that they give up time to engage with these small groups of associates; they're really building relationships with folks they wouldn't otherwise interact with on a daily basis.

I was honored to be nominated to the first U.S. LBM class at the University of Tennessee's accelerated-learning program (now called Pulse). I received numerous helpful tips and strategies from the UT professors that I use daily to help me run the business at Lyman Roofing & Siding (LRS). I also enjoyed the camaraderie and interaction with my fellow classmates; the time spent discussing targeting and service strategies needed to expand into the R&R segment were extremely helpful for me. Although there were many great experiences that I took away from the program, my favorite and most helpful was the mentoring program. At first I was disappointed that Wendy would pair me up with Doug Jones (a huge Chicago Bears fan); I wasn't sure this relationship would work. Well after a few conversations and putting our football differences aside, I realized Doug was a perfect fit as my mentor. Doug's positive attitude, outlook on the industry, and his passion to innovate made him a perfect mentor for me. Doug and I had weekly calls where we discussed numerous topics: hiring, budgeting, and technology are only a few. He also suggested different management books and articles to read throughout the mentorship program that would help me gain a different perspective. Doug was a HUGE resource for me as I was opening up the new LRS facility, because he explained to me the pain points and struggles he had when opening his new locations. I am glad I was chosen for the learning opportunity, and at the end of the day, I am extremely happy Wendy teamed me up with Doug (even though he is a Bears fan)!

— Collin Owens
branch manager, Lyman Roofing and Siding

Many participants say it's a real eye-opening experience. They often comment how rare it is to see the entire executive group sit down six times a year with groups of twenty people and really talk to them one-on-one about why we believe what we believe. They want to know what they need to do differently going forward, and we address that by telling stories of associates who've already moved the needle in our company. Through the stories, they get a glimpse of what's possible.

During the workshop, we talk a lot about *failing more*. I tell them that, as a company, we don't fail enough. When we don't fail enough, we're not trying enough new things to innovate our business. We have an open discussion about where we're playing it too safe.

The demand to attend the classes is high, and training is offered off-site regionally. That's also part of the magic. People in different positions are brought in from different companies and they start to develop relationships through networking. Ongoing communication outside the program is then greatly encouraged. In fact, there are several success stories where even after the classroom time, people continued to get together and visit other branches to share best practices.

In addition to the in-person training and development sessions, U.S. LBM has invested in a software platform that allows for internal networking and collaboration on specific learning objectives.

MOMENTUM IS ADDICTING

Since one of the key tenants of our company is how we treat our people, then we owe it to them to provide them with tools and resources. And they haven't let us down; our front-line associates can help us accelerate faster by sharing their ideas and observations. We're very impressed our people and local teams and their ability to grow with us and help us achieve success. Once you go down this path of building people up, driving change, and positively impacting an entire industry community, you want more. You want to see just how far you can go. Watching the people grow and learn and move forward is the most rewarding part of any business.

When you have a company that has our kind of mandate—to get better in every aspect—you create a constant need to develop people to drive the growth and fill the future needs of the company. The best way to do that is to do it yourself. It may seem like a daunting, expensive task. But really, there's just no other way to do it than to develop the people.

And once associates see one or two of their colleagues go through this program and lead projects and see benefits, it's contagious. Everybody wants to be a part of it. Consequently, the momentum we're experiencing in our company is addicting.

We've had hundreds of graduates of the program, creating an army of people who constantly challenge everything about our business and who try to find new and better ways to do things. Today, we have nearly three hundred certified Lean Six Sigma Yellow Belts across our company and sixty certified Green Belts who lead continuous improvement projects in addition to their full-time jobs in sales, operations, or supply chain. We have thirty-five aspiring leaders who have completed a year-long accelerated professional development program, including immersion learning at the University of Tennessee, leadership assessments, one-on-one coaching, and mentorship. And over 230 associates representing all levels and functions of the organization have attended the two-day U.S. LBM University workshop led by me and our executive team. Those are pretty exciting numbers—numbers that we will continue to grow.

CHAPTER 9

EVERYDAY ACTS
OF COURAGE

Going back to our childhood, we all used to try new things until we got it right. Then, we'd go on to the next thing. Somehow along the way, we forgot about that basic child-like instinct. We started to assume that, in business, all decisions have to be perfect or we're in trouble. Or, if our decision turned out to be imperfect, that we'd be judged and others would look down on us. I believe we've got to celebrate failures in business and learn from them. We have to eradicate the fear of failure in our people and celebrate risk-takers who are open to change.

Most leaders, including people in our industry, typically work hard to get promoted and earn more responsibility and more money. Eventually they may even earn their way to the very top. Once they get there, obviously they don't want to lose that job, so the safest thing to do is everything that's been done in the past. Often, they just follow in the footsteps of the person who had the job for before them, because that creates a comfort zone of sameness and a tendency to continue to maintain status quo. They make very safe decisions because they don't want to take risk; they want to stay under the radar so no one pays much attention to them. It's very rare that somebody comes up through the ranks of a company and really has visions of wanting to change the company or the culture or the entire industry.

Similarly, companies tend to put the most experienced people in charge of businesses. Often that means a person has spent a lot of years in the industry, so he or she has fewer years left. Especially if that new leader is not visionary, and is less likely to see the long-term results of being innovative, then he or she may only focus on short-term results and just getting through the next two, three, four, or five years.

We're the opposite. Experience and age don't necessarily define leaders in our organization. We look for people who differentiate themselves, people who kind of rise up naturally up from inside our organization. We also hire from the outside, from other industries. But when it comes to people who fit the culture and who can really excel in a culture like ours—where they're encouraged to take chances, try new things, and really find the next big idea—I think those people rise from the associates we currently have onboard.

While we want everyone to care and be engaged, we really only need a handful of people who really want to change themselves, their location, their market, their company, and the industry. It's about the law of averages: If we send two hundred associates to Yellow Belt training, we're not delusional enough to think all two hundred will be aggressive and go out and jump on projects. But, if a quarter of the two hundred run with a challenge, it's a good return on investment and a success story for the entire organization.

Once we identify those potential leaders in our organization, then we start taking them through some of our best-in-class leadership-training programs. In addition to leadership training, these programs also introduce participants to different concepts from different industries and different areas of the country. We want them to think "bigger picture"—to not just look inwardly for innovation and change, but to look for best practices from other businesses as well. As R. Hunter Morin, the president and founder of The GeMROI Co., explains:

> In this industry, no company has committed as many resources to training and education of current and future leaders within the company as U.S. LBM has. This is an incredible example for an industry where no formal training program existed.

Our proprietary leadership-development course was developed internally but is conducted with the help of the University of Tennessee, Knoxville. Known as "Pulse," this program is geared toward emerging leaders, the next generation of people we believe will lead our organization. We call the program Pulse because we view these aspiring leaders as the pulse of our organization in the future. So we make significant investment in that group of folks who are on the path to take on senior-leadership roles down the road.

Pulse is a yearlong program that is a combination of different types of training and experiences. It includes immersion learning, where participants go to the University of Tennessee in Knoxville and sit through six days of classroom learning. Then participants go through a series of leadership assessments. They each have a one-on-one coaching session and they put together formal action plans for their own professional development. Then they are paired up with a mentor in the organization but outside of their market—somebody in a different part of the organization who helps them work specifically on the action plan that they designed as part of their participation in this class.

NO COWBOYS

Think about leadership in the old days in which cowboys drove the cattle herd forward. They could only go as fast as the stragglers, so the average or the status quo is what held them back. For us, the better method is to take the best people we have and the best group we have and explain to them exactly where we're going and then tell them to run like hell to get there—the rest of the herd is going to follow them. There are no cowboys needed in our model.

We commonly talk in our company about courageous leadership. Part of the definition of courageous leadership is to lead by example. We're not afraid to share our mistakes. We're not afraid to talk about things that are working really well and things that aren't working. It's never personal. It's always about what we're doing.

And we must practice what we preach as executives. In the executive-level group, we must be very honest about our own mistakes and how we talk. Removing ego from the process is an unbelievably important step because ego leads to defensiveness which, in turn, stifles creativity and innovation. Taking that ego out of the equation allows people to realize that, even leaders are real people who make mistakes.

FAILURE IS AN OPTION

As I've mentioned, we really try to create a culture where it's okay to fail, because even when we fail, we learn so much. These lessons help us the next time we need to adjust to fix a same or similar problem, because we know so much more than we did before.

So we go the next level with our thoughts and actions. Instead of maintaining the status quo, we think we've got to challenge thoughts and try new ideas. We've got to take risks. We don't mind people trying new things that don't work out. At the end of the day, all we care about is whether we got better, whether we learned something, and whether we are better today than we were yesterday.

And we really do learn from everything we do. Even if we fail or don't get the outcome we expected, we always learn something along the way, which helps us make a much better decision the next time. That doesn't mean we're careless and reckless. It really means that we are willing to try new things.

Again, if you really want to change things and be progressive, you've got to have an environment where people are not afraid to make mistakes. So from the beginning of the onboarding process, we teach new associates that it's okay to make mistakes; it's okay to fail. We don't judge people when they are willing to take risks. I believe that message starts with me setting the example, and the approach works because we invest a lot of time in the interview process to ensure we hire the right people.

In order to get past the fear of failure, we need to try to understand root causes. For example, I'm confident the investment in a customer mobile app is the "right risk" because I feel like we understand our customer very well. What gives me continued confidence is that we have an organization that's really good at changing. So even if we go down a road and we find out that we're 90 percent there with a project or idea, but we can't make it work in the end, we'll be able to change and make use of that 90 percent that *did* work while trying the project or idea from a different perspective. We'll still be able to create value, even if we have to change direction late in the game. And even if it was a complete failure, we learn so much along the way that the next time we go at it, we're sure to get it that much more right because of the time, energy, and effort we invested today.

You can't afford not to fail, because people are going to blow by you at such a rate. Whenever a company goes out of business, I wonder if the leader asks him or herself, "Maybe I could have afforded a little more risk?"

Leaders should learn to be okay with spending some money and failing on a project, but then learning from that experience and doing it better the next time around. Even things you succeed at become obsolete at a faster rate today than in the past. Don't think of an ERP expense, for example, as a one-time expense. View it as an every-year expense to continue your education, a tuition of sorts that will continue to make you better and better, that will equip you to be fearless at taking bold leaps into things that really can add efficiency or differentiate you or create more of a value proposition. If you're willing to invest—not only your money but also in your people and their common effort—it just becomes part of the organization.

In our annual meeting, we give away awards for people who move the needle the most inside our company. These are not only the people who came up with the great ideas or a new way to do something that really changed and made our company better. It might also be a great idea or somebody who really stepped out of their comfort level to try something new. Maybe it didn't work, but maybe it created something better. We spend a lot of time talking through stories about how not everything that we do turns out exactly the way we thought it would. But sometimes the result is still pretty notable.

It's a little like when the 3M Post-it note was invented. They didn't set up to invest in a sticky note; they were trying to make a stronger glue. What they came up with instead was a glue that never dried and could be peeled off without any residue. And the rest is history.

If we don't encourage mistakes, then we're never going to encourage progress either.

HIDDEN LEADERS

Leadership is not defined by a title in our company. (We even kick around the idea of how to get rid of titles.)

At our core, we see ourselves as a people-first company that is passionate about continuous improvement. It's instinctive that we want to improve every key metric across the board. I have sometime been surprised by people already inside our organization who had hidden talents we'd never suspected. When offered the right opportunity, you may suddenly see people already on your team in a new light. If you can create a culture that really lets people feel safe and where they can put themselves out there and try new things and be innovative, you might find that you have a lot more leader types already on your payroll.

In fact, we find passionate associates in all types of positions across the company who embrace change and who can lead improvements in our business. It's like the Yellow Belt certified CDL driver who helped change the layout of his yard and reduced truck-turnaround time. He doesn't sit at the boardroom level, but he has significantly impacted the business just the same. That's the opportunity open to each and every one of our associates across the country—to make a significant impact.

We give away awards at our annual meeting, and two of the recent awardees were actually two of the newer managers who were not only new to our company but new to the industry. They received the awards for ideas that they brought from those other industries. Maybe they were a little more open-minded, but to us, it was a constant reminder that you've got to hire the right people to create the culture that you want. You've got to have a mix of the old as well as the new.

APPROPRIATE RISK

There are several ways to think about how we take risk in our organization.

When we're talking about big projects like Lean Six Sigma, the connotation is along the lines of bigger acts of courage that could have an impact over multiple locations or on revenue across the organization.

When we meet with associates in small groups, or when we meet with an acquisition team for the first time, we also talk about everyday acts of courage. We talk about creating a work environment where there's a level of trust, where people at all levels of the organization feel confident that they can speak their minds if they see a better way to do things, and where they have a voice that allows them to bring ideas or concerns forward without being chastised for being the outlier or fearing that their input will fall on deaf ears.

We talk to new supervisors and managers about their roles in providing opportunities that push their direct reports into their discomfort zone. We also talk to them about new and different assignments for their own professional growth. We call these everyday acts of courage. We're trying to drive a mindset that's about being willing to take risk and take action, but it's also just about being willing to speak your mind and be yourself. It's about bringing your best to work every day and not hesitating share big ideas because of some sort of hierarchy that exists.

Ours is the kind of culture where people can toss out ideas and brainstorm openly. The brainstorming generates lively discussion and challenges us to see different sides of an idea. Everyone is invited to weigh in with a pro or con to help shape the idea, regardless of their job title or status. Ideas can come from anyone or any location. If it's a valid idea, a team is formed to move the project forward.

So we want everyone in our organization to actively engage in conversation about the next big idea we can invent. We're going to take rifle shots across different groups, and we're going to make a ton of mistakes, but that's okay. There is definitely a vetting process where we talk about what we want to try and where we want to try it. Where's the best location to give that idea a good chance for success? With more than two hundred locations, we're going to try new things in an isolated market to understand how it works and get customer reactions. If we fail on seven, eight, or nine of those out of ten, that's okay, because we're going to hit one thing where we say, "Wow. This is a game changer!" Then we can immediately take that idea, product, or service to the other 190-plus locations and show them how it works, and from there it should be quickly implemented.

COMMUNICATING THE VISION

Leaders need to communicate the vision and provide the resources to be successful—though sometimes they should step aside and let associates have at it.

At our annual meeting, which includes all of the managers in all the functional areas —around three hundred people—we talk about the past year. We celebrate wins, discuss losses, and reset for the next year. The meeting is usually held in conjunction with the National Association of Home Builders International Builders Show, which gives us a great chance to get out and meet with our vendors and customers. Our people leave feeling pretty energized about where the company's going and what we're about; it really helps set the tone for the coming year and helps us prioritize and foster enthusiasm and alignment.

As an organization rife with ideas and driven to plow full speed ahead, we know we're often out there on the cutting edge of change. As such, all leaders sometimes have to say things they don't necessarily even believe themselves. Maybe you've got a vision for some project that is actually impossible. But if you can get everyone else to buy into that vision—to believe that it's possible until they realize it isn't—then they will learn a lot along the way. They will see how far they can really go before it's decided that you're going another direction instead.

If we always knew exactly where we were going, we would all probably manage business the same way. But I personally think that would be a little boring. I think it's exciting that we don't know exactly what the next great technology or the next great game changer is going to be. That way we all get a chance when it happens to see how well we can implement and integrate it into our company. Rather than a company where associates must guess at what's ahead, I believe we've created a company that readily adapts to change. Regardless of what changes are on the horizon, we're very good at implementing them. We're very good at change and at communicating those changes.

Our people believe in our vision because they live it. And the more they embrace it, the more they see that it adds to their success and to the success of the people around them. I think there are a lot of lessons in there. One is that all people work to feed their families and make a living. But once you achieve a role in management, you stop thinking as much about your own income and other personal priorities, and, instead, you try to support and make the people around you the best *they* can be. At that point, all of that comes back to you in return, and you end up being more successful than you ever thought possible. In essence, you really do succeed through other people.

At its core, I believe leadership is the ability to paint a vision that people can understand and then inspire them to follow. In the old days, maybe a leader was a boss who could give you an assignment and nudge you along the way and lead you to the answer. Today, we paint the vision of where we want to go, and then we invite our 4,500-plus associates to help us find a way to get there—to create a new path. The corporate team doesn't have all the answers, and in our model we're not expected to have all the answers. But we've got something even better than an answer book; we've got a talented and engaged team of leaders who will communicate the vision down through the markets and locations, and then facilitate a two-way conversation on how to solve the most complex business challenges of today. An effective leader will communicate the vision well, both up and down the organization, so that it becomes an energy or call to action rather than just words on the company website.

CHAPTER 10

FINDING A CULTURAL FIT

Accelerating our culture is thoughtfully woven into our acquisition strategy.

We have some key indicators we look for in every acquisition. One of the most important is: How does a company fit into the organization? Can we make the target company better, and can they make us better? Will we function well together? That's where big companies can start breaking down—when they bring in people whose vision is inconsistent with what they're trying to drive. Don't misunderstand this important point: diverse viewpoints and ideas are an asset to becoming a stronger company. But, if we have philosophically different views of the end game, gaining alignment could become a debilitating distraction. You must have everybody really aligned and headed in the right direction.

Partnering with the right companies in our model is very important and we spend a lot of time on that end to make sure it all makes sense and that the organization being acquired buys into what we're trying to do.

When looking for potential acquisitions, we look at, obviously, past results: How has the company managed through cycles, and how successful has it been? We look at the culture and the personalities of the people who run the company: Do they let the market dictate success?

Have they been able to overcome certain things? What things are they the best at? What's their market share?

All those things are easy to quantify, but they're actually not the most important ingredients to success in the future or in our models. Again, that comes down to *people*.

When I go out to visit a potential acquisition target, obviously I pay a lot of attention to the people. I look at the ownership and whether it has the right personality and the right makeup to excel in our culture. I also pay a lot of attention to the people right underneath that layer and the people in the more functional areas—does the organization have the kind of people who are going to really embrace new, better, different?

So I pay a lot of attention to the personalities and the people that are in that company to see how they're going to react. Often, after a company joins us, we go out and meet with the people in the acquired company. We meet with every person and we tell him or her our culture and our vision. And we start challenging them to think differently from day one.

When you're performing acquisitions at a rate like we are, you have to be very intentional about driving the culture and making sure it doesn't get watered down or lost," Wendy Whiteash, U.S. LBM vice president of strategy and organizational development told a report for *Modern Distribution Management*. "The executive team is on-site at the acquired business (the first week or two) to meet with all associates, to welcome them, tell the U.S. LBM story, and make a personal connection ... We're bringing on companies that have their own histories, their own perspectives and cultures... Minimizing the emotional changes that typically come with acquisitions is also important as we begin to grow a trusting relationship with the newly acquired team. We're clear up front that there is no intention to change the operating company's name or leadership team.[1]

---

1 Jenel Stelton-Holtmeier, "M&A: Easing the Transition," *Modern Distribution Management*, 45, no. 18 (2015).

Sometimes people get it in the first meeting. Sometimes it takes a little time. Sometimes, we have to send some people through a few other trainings. And it's an amazing thing to watch the lights go on and people say, "I've always thought that maybe if we tried this it would work, but we've never had the resources to do so." That's the kind of attitude we look for in a company. We want people who are going to embrace what we do, who are going to thrive in our culture. I think that's what makes our company different.

As I've said, we think the next great idea can come from anyone in the company. It can come from a truck driver, a forklift driver, a salesperson, or an accounting clerk. That next great idea, the next big change, or the next thing that will give us a competitive advantage or increase our value to our customers and our vendors, can come from anywhere in the company. We've learned that, and we embrace that, and I think people want to be part of that.

WHAT MAKES YOU DIFFERENT?

We don't really look for business turnarounds; we definitely look for the market leaders who have a history of success. They have a history of winning. It's a big part of the culture that we want to establish. We tend to find the personality traits that we're looking for in the people who are number one and number two in their markets more than the others.

We actually do quite a few acquisitions, so we interview quite a few acquisition candidates, and the first question I typically ask is, "What makes you different than everybody else in the market?" It's kind of comical, but the answers are always the same: "service." Everybody feels like they differentiate their business on service. When you ask them to further expand on that, they'll explain how they've gone the "extra mile" by making a delivery in their personal vehicle, or how their location manager will come in to open the yard at all hours to address a customer emergency. All the answers are pretty much the same.

If the company says, "Service is what makes us different," we know how to put metrics to some of the things that the company does. It's one thing to think you're good at something, but it's another to see the numbers behind it. I think a lot of times our acquisition targets are surprised—things that maybe they thought they were really good at reveal some metrics that aren't that great, but things they didn't pay that much attention to may reveal some very good metrics.

The companies we acquire are somewhat different because they're leaders—but something *made* them a leader. They're usually very good at something, whether it's process, or selling, or getting new customers, or pushing new products. They always have a strength. What we try to do is amplify that strength. If it's something we can do in the rest of the organization, that's great. Just like any company, there are always weaknesses in the organizations we acquire as well. And our strength is that we bring in some best practices to help shore those up.

It really is about looking at the business and saying, "Yeah, we don't want to change the things you guys are really good at. We don't want to change the culture. What we want to do is bring you resources to help you guys get better at other things." Usually those things are smaller, because whatever that team is talented at, that's typically where the company has put it efforts.

There's always something that gets missed or some opportunity to get better, and every company always has those opportunities. It's our job to identify them and find the best practices to plug those holes.

As a tendency, people and organizations always want to get better. They always want to feel like they're winning. A big part of our business is first defining what winning looks like. Another is showing them the information that lets them see how they're performing, which lets them make decisions on ways they can improve. We give them the tools to create an environment that is collaborative and positive—one that people like to work in. I really believe everybody wants to feel like they contribute during the day—they want to feel what it's like to win. We just try to create the environment where that's possible.

Of course, we always analyze the markets that we're going into. We don't have a set strategy on the exact geography. But obviously, we want to be in markets where we feel like we have a successful future. Instead, it's mostly the company and the team itself that really gets us interested in an acquisition, making sure it's a good fit for us and for them—because, again, we don't like to change the management team. It's just not part of our motto. We want to partner with people who stay with the business, who want to continue to grow the business and be part of the future. Maybe it's a long-term succession plan. Maybe it's just taking some money off the table. Whatever might be the reason for selling, we want to make sure we continue to partner with the team that's already been successful and then try to let them focus on the things they love, like growing the business, spending more time with customers, or bringing new products to the market.

The people we partner with are very good at managing their businesses. If they're going to make decisions, more often than not they're going to make them much faster if they don't have to run up and down the food chain. So we let them continue to make those decisions. If we disagree, we can guide them later, but I would rather make a bad decision quickly than take a long time to make a good decision. We can make the wrong decisions, see the outcomes, and then fix what didn't work probably faster than most people will make the first decision. And that's okay. I think making mistakes is part of life, and as I've said, it's part of our business, and we don't mind that. We'd rather be fast than be careful just to always be right.

Lyman Companies' president Dale Carlson, talks about the uniqueness of our culture:

> The U.S. LBM culture is uniquely different than most large companies in that it is autonomous to the nth degree. Corporate offers many resources and acts more like a business consultant, so it's up to local leadership to decide what to implement, when, and

how. It's an environment where strong independent leaders can thrive.

Once a company becomes part of U.S. LBM, we take some of the back-office pieces that the company wasn't as good at or didn't enjoy doing into our central office. But all the things that need to be local—the relationships, the processes, and anything that helps customers—remain local.

I think we bring some great distribution and systems technology to the table. We certainly want to put those in over time. But we try to fully assess what any changes might mean before we just assume and implement. We're not in a rush to go in and drop a new ERP system in the first month of the business. We'll slowly migrate, if it makes sense to do so. The good thing is we typically have a newer version of probably the most common systems that are already in the industry. Usually that's a very minimal change over time. The rest of it, as we look to integrate and have them become part of us, really is about adopting the U.S. LBM culture into their culture. Again, that's a culture of continuous improvement, of using our resources, of being open to change. It's a very, very collaborative environment.

As of the writing of this book, we have done around forty acquisitions. And those forty acquisitions are really forty good commercials for telling prospective acquisitions that we do what we say we're going to do! As I said, we don't change the meaningful pieces of a company. We only do things that enhance and add value. We really do try to maximize the value of being a local independent, while also bringing in the buying power and energy of a large organization. I think *that*, in a nutshell, is what makes it attractive for potential acquisitions—and for us to want to partner with them.

CHAPTER 11

WE TAKE OUR ROLE
VERY SERIOUSLY

We take our role as a change leader seriously.

When we created U.S. LBM, it wasn't to build a big distributor in this space. It was to build a new and different company that focuses on things a little differently. Some of the things we've done, quite frankly, we did just to make sure we reminded our own people we're different.

For example, we're constantly looking at better ways to manage the data and information in our business, and I think there's a day coming fairly soon when we'll all be able to transfer information much more quickly and efficiently. That might level the playing field even more, but I see it as the opposite—I think there's a real opportunity there. If you're the best at managing information, then stakeholders above and below you in the supply chain will come to you for knowledge. And your business will have extremely loyal customers and vendors.

So our approach is different, but I think when you talk about competitive advantage, culture in itself is the biggest competitive advantage because it makes your associates feel that they belong, that they're connected to the company. As a result, they engage. To me that is the biggest advantage anybody can have.

Craig Webb, editor-in-chief of *Remodeling* and *ProSales* magazines, aptly describes our culture:

> The closest parallel to U.S. LBM's corporate culture that I can think of is the European Union in its earliest days. Just after World War II, a handful of nations voluntarily committed themselves to create a common market and a shared way to operate. It was a coalition of the willing, in which the leaders of the group weren't so much executives as they were recognized visionaries with a consistent, compelling message.
>
> I sensed all that when I attended a meeting of U.S. LBM's unit presidents. The presidents' body language was respectful of L.T. but not deferential. I got no sense that people were frightened of the boss or kowtowing to him. And the attitude displayed by L.T. and the other executive-level staff was collegial and helpful: "We want to help you be the best that you can be." With an atmosphere like that, who wouldn't want to take part?

More than most operations, we put a higher reliance on technology and on open-book management. We are going to change at a rate faster than the industry, as fast as technology will take us, so by setting benchmarks and showing how operations compare, there's a natural inclination by the presidents—who all are born competitors—toward using best practices to get ahead.

Our own supply chain executive vice president, Randy Aardema, confirmed Webb's description of my management style, describing me as "not a manager at all." He said:

> L.T. paints a vision of what he expects, and he's clear about what he wants. But at the same time, he isn't publicly critical of any of the corporate presidents. He never gets mad at people. Instead he tells them: "Here's where we have to improve."

BUT SERIOUSLY FOLKS ...

We take our reputation very seriously. In the beginning, we were often viewed as a holding company that was simply the sums of its parts without real synergies or alignment. But, look at us now.

In 2014, we were the fastest-growing distributor for each of our vendor partners. Those vendors see us as an avenue to grow, and they add value to us by helping us be competitive. We view our chain as very holistic in how we work with all of them, the people in the channel, to make everyone more efficient, while giving them more knowledge about where things are. That's really, I think, the difference in the future of the business; it's about how everybody can work together to make the channel as efficient as possible.

We also believe we have the opportunity to raise the bar for the whole industry, one in which little has changed for the past hundred years. But our industry is now at a critical point in time where technology, the economy, the political landscape, and other factors, are presenting us with the impetus for dramatic changes. And our company's built-in discipline and ability to change is, and will continue to be, a competitive advantage in the evolution that certainly lies ahead.

It's no longer about just buying in bulk and breaking down units and taking all that to the jobsite. It's about offering solutions to our customers beyond just the delivery of products. It's about product selection. It's about determining how much product is needed on a jobsite. It's about helping customers understand the differences between the qualities of various products and how things are going to function in certain environments. In short, it's a far different world.

Our January 2015 annual meeting slogan was "Accelerating at the Speed of US." It was our five-year anniversary and an opportunity to stop and celebrate all the accomplishments we've made in those first five years. Not only did we celebrate the past, but, we spent ample time looking toward the future. The slogan was a call to action. It called for everyone's buy-in to help move us forward and continue to transform the business, rather than sit back and wait for a select few leaders to drive us forward.

Preparing for the five-year celebration was a good time for me to reflect on our progress and the decisions the team and I have made, which have subsequently shaped what the company is today. I'm often asked, "Looking back, what were the key decision points that helped U.S. LBM gain such a strong foothold so quickly?" To be honest, there were quite a few decisions made early to which I can attribute our success today. Among these are the core values that we formulated and documented early on, including staying true to being a people-first company. In our brief history, we've also overcome a lot of the doubters who didn't believe our corporate structure (no corporate office) would work. The decision to be firm on our acquisitions strategy—to partner with people that fit our culture and our model—may sound intangible or fluffy, but that was another key decision early on that has certainly impacted our success trajectory in the pro-dealer market today.

Our story is certainly not about one person. It's not about a small group of people. It's about all of us. That was the message at the annual meeting. "Accelerating at the Speed of US" means that we control our destiny at this point, because we control the rate at which we change. We drive the change and are not victims of change. It's an unbelievably powerful position to be in.

More importantly, it may have taken thirty, forty, or fifty years to make the last change for some of these companies, but the next ones are not going to take that long. We're going to be something totally different and much faster in the future. The ability to change and to have a structure in your company that allows you to change at a faster rate than others is going to be a big advantage going forward.

I do think there is potential for organizations to grow too fast. However, our existing model, resources, and strategy provide us with the opportunity to aggressively expand and successfully manage this growth. We analyze market data on a daily basis in search of additional opportunities to benefit U.S. LBM as a whole. Due to our structure, we have the unique opportunity to partner with some of the best companies in the industry. Our competitors are not in the position to do the same. Taking market share and expansion is essential for each of our respective companies to remain healthy and reach their potential.

To stay centered on what's most important from day to day, I focus on the people—the people who've been around me before U.S. LBM existed and the people in our company today. I'm constantly learning from these people; they teach me something new each and every day. We don't have preconceived ideas about what this company can become or what it should become. Together, we learn as we go, and I feel challenged every day. I think as long as we stay true to ourselves—that we're a people-first company, that we want to get better, that our culture is very important—and as long as we stay true to those pieces while keeping close watch over our customers' needs, then the sky's the limit for what we can become.

My job is one of the easiest in the company; I make sure I challenge the way people think. Sometimes I even throw some off-the-wall idea that may be impossible just to get us to think about things in a different light. But, the team is composed of the people who really make everything happen.

So needless to say, I love what I do. Like Mark Twain said, "The secret of success is making your vocation your vacation." My job is a lot of fun, and we've got a great group of people, and they're a pleasure to work with every day.

There's a lot of uncertainty about what the future really looks like in our industry, so we need to constantly reinvent ourselves. From the U.S. LBM point of view, we're very happy that the future is a little gray and a little cloudy. Because what we've done rather than just say, "This is what our industry will look like in 2030," we've built a unique model and culture that says we can change at a faster rate than anybody else. At least we feel like we're nimble, like we can adapt at a rapid pace. And we feel like we're very good at taking the newest and latest and making it into a simple solution that works and enhances our customers' businesses and thus enhances our value proposition. That's really what gives us confidence going forward—that we'll be able to continue to change with the industry or maybe even get out in front and make the industry change a little bit along the way ourselves. The truth is, we're just getting started!

How are you at embracing change? Change and continuous improvement are an important part of our progressive, forward-thinking company. If you feel that you are aligned with our ideas, with our culture, with our way changing our industry and the world, then we invite you to join us!

TESTIMONIALS

"Our corporate culture fosters individual and team empowerment, ownership, and a liberating fearlessness to swing out and be creative. It's a compelling environment unlike any other in our industry, and that gives U.S. LBM a real competitive advantage."

Henry Rosehill, product line manager,
roofing and siding, U.S. LBM

"What I value most about my corporate culture is that my CEO responds to me when I ask him a question, and he tells us it's okay to fail because that is one of the ways to make a person successful—if they learn from what/why they failed."

Jim Sullivan, director of
purchasing, commodities, U.S. LBM

"US LBM has reinvented the four P's of the marketing mix for building materials; **P**rograms (aggregated power), **P**rocess (improvement), **P**ractices (best) and **P**eople (empowered)!"

Tim Leister, president, Lyman Companies

"We are creating self-aware employees that can make decisions in a timely fashion not weighted down by old, outdated chain-of-command structures. Our customers benefit greatly from this way of doing business. They save time and are not inconvenienced or aggravated by employees not having answers when they need them. I also believe empowering employees creates an environment of teamwork."

Anthony DeCesero, branch manager,
Universal Supply Company

"Many companies are all about the customer (so they say) but not the employee. This has always been backwards to me. By making the employee feel important, not only by saying the words but living them out as U.S. LBM does, it creates a trust that I'm not sure other companies enjoy."

Dale Eggers, president, Desert Trust Financial Group

"We receive help from corporate resources—as an example our PLMs—that help us as partners, not as dictators. Other departments, such as HR, finance, and training and development, have all responded to any of our requests for assistance as if we are in this together—as one team. "

Nick Berardis, president, East Haven Builders Supply

"Not only do they maintain the comforts and entrepreneurial aspects of working for their original employer, but they gain the benefits of having the resources and security of a multi-billion dollar organization. The largest benefactor is the customer, who benefits from improved supply-chain strategy, continuous process improvement, and increased value propositions that a small business could not provide operating by itself.

It is truly the best of both worlds combined to make each entity stronger and more sustainable."

Seth Teitelbaum, vice president,
Direct Cabinet Sales, Inc.

"Our culture of empowerment is like crowd sourcing; everyone who wants to contribute has a voice."

Melora Spriggs, human resource
information system manager, U.S. LBM

"The road to continuous improvement and innovation is paved by our culture of 'fail fast and learn.'"

Charlie Bradburn, branch manager,
ABC Millwork & Cabinetry

"Joining U.S. LBM has afforded me the opportunity to take my career to the next level. I have had the opportunity to dive in to new areas that I did not previously have exposure to, such as: acquisitions, talent development, succession planning, and the ability to take a best practice and share it with another division and see the improvements recognized on the other end. If there is something that I am interested in becoming involved in, all I have to do is ask."

Andrea Berg, human resources manager,
Lyman Companies

"The culture and structure of U.S. LBM is the foundation of autonomy within the individual operating companies. This core concept promotes respect and partnership, encouraging each business unit to work closely with the PLMs to drive success through innovative thought and shared best practices."

Tiffany Reeder, product line manager,
cabinetry, U.S. LBM

"Everyone is aware of the adage "there is strength in numbers," and as U.S. LBM has grown, we have just begun to see the benefits of our size in our relationships with our vendors. The great thing about U.S. LBM is that the Opcos can join forces to realize benefits together but also maintain their own identities within the Opcos."

Kenneth Feldman, president, Feldman Lumber

"In an industry filled with well-read people who can recite buzz words and catchphrases, the difference with U.S. LBM is that 'We Live It.'"

Mark Francis, vice president, Shelly Enterprises

"I'm looking to put my professional career on steroids, and I truly believe that U.S. LBM is committed to helping me achieve that goal."

Patrick Wetzel, outside sales representative, Hines Supply

"U.S. LBM provides me as an associate the best of both worlds: the power of a large company and the family feel of a small organization. I know that my personal and professional development is a priority, and I value the fact that the experts are accessible."

Katie Gulotta, human resources manager, Shelly's Supply

"U.S. LBM differentiates itself from the competition by living up to its mission statement/core values each and every day. We have a dedicated, passionate, and talented team that truly cares about each other. By providing leadership, development, and an open-door environment to our associates, they feel empowered and appreciated."

Karen Charielle, vice president
of human resources, U.S. LBM

"Doing the same old thing is not acceptable with U.S. LBM. In order to continue to grow you must do something—doing nothing is not acceptable."

Greg Yarmesch, area operations manager,
Coastal Roofing Supply

"At U.S. LBM, I admire the focus on continuous process improvement, the latitude to make mistakes (and of course learn from them), as well as the autonomy that's allowed at the location level to manage the business to the customer's expectations and to competitive influences within the market."

Kevin King, general manager,
Wisconsin Building Supply

"The people working for our corporate team are to be used as a resource; they are not there to tell you that you need to do things just because they are the smartest people in the room. The corporate philosophy is more 'We are all in this together. What can we do to help?' Now that's refreshing."

Mike Lombardi, logistics manager, U.S. LBM

"The entrepreneurial culture within U.S. LBM that starts from our fundamental business model and is fully supported up into senior management is a strategic advantage in many ways. It allows us to have the speed and flexibility in our local markets that companies our size typically just can't match."

Greg Gaskell, president, Bellevue Builders Supply

"Decision making, as it relates to customers at the local level, and a lean management structure are key difference makers for us. We can quickly make business decisions that impact the street."

Bob Materazzi, Jr., sales manager, Universal Supply Company

"The lumber and building-material distribution industry is centered on relationships. I'm proud to be part of an organization that values the relationships we hold with our customers, vendors, associates, and our community. U.S. LBM goes above and beyond to ensure the strength of these relationships and provides the tools to help us all develop them deeper."

Gregory Bossert, vice president
of information systems, U.S. LBM

"I value the U.S. LBM 'freedom and flexibility to be GREAT' culture that empowers its associates by encouraging healthy risk, providing resources, best practices, and learning and growth opportunities!"

Lawanna Dendy, vice president of administration,
GBS Building Supply, Inc.

Printed in the USA
CPSIA information can be obtained
at www.ICGtesting.com
JSHW012055140824
68134JS00035B/3458